Uncle Tom's Journey
from Maryland to Canada

Uncle Tom's Journey

from Maryland to Canada

The Life of Josiah Henson

To Beverly,

Thanks for your interest and support for this unsung hero!

Edna

Edna M. Troiano

Edna M. Troiano

THE
History
PRESS

Published by The History Press
Charleston, SC
www.historypress.com

First published 2019

Manufactured in the United States

ISBN 9781625859419

Library of Congress Control Number: 2018958999

Dedicated to all those who keep Josiah Henson's memory alive.

CONTENTS

PREFACE

In the summer of 2016, my friend Sonja Scharles, knowing my fascination with archaeology, invited me to visit La Grange, a historic home in La Plata, Maryland, where Dr. Julia King of St. Mary's College of Maryland and her students were excavating, looking for evidence of the birthplace of Josiah Henson.

Dr. King explained to me that Josiah Henson, who had been born only a few miles from my home, had escaped from slavery, founded a settlement and a school in Canada, was reputed to be the model for Uncle Tom in Harriet Beecher Stowe's novel *Uncle Tom's Cabin*, had rescued people via the Underground Railroad, and had been renowned in American and England for his sermons and lectures. Stunned, I asked, "Why haven't I ever heard of him?" King replied, "That's what everybody says."

I have a doctorate in literature, have taught African American literature, read the slave narratives, and am well informed about the history of slavery, yet I had never heard of Henson. Like many writers, I had found a story that wouldn't leave me alone. I continued to mull over his life. But part of my fascination was not strictly with Henson's life—it was also with his disappearance from history. When students learned about Frederick Douglass and Harriet Tubman, why didn't they also learn about Josiah Henson?

When I mentioned to Keenan Holmes, a museum docent at the Josiah Henson Special Park in Montgomery County, Maryland, that I was thinking about writing about Henson, he pointed out that Henson had already written his autobiography and asked what I had to add. It seemed to me that there were two large pieces missing from the story: why Henson's fame had faded and what efforts were being made to educate people about him.

In addition to retelling the life of this remarkable man, I decided to investigate how Henson's relationship with Stowe's Uncle Tom both enhanced and diminished his fame and to explore the sites where he lived. As William Faulkner famously said, "The past isn't dead; it isn't even past." In tracing Henson from Maryland to Kentucky to Canada, I discovered sites devoted to Henson and met people dedicated to educating the public about his life. Their goal, like mine, is to reinstate Henson as the hero he was once known to be.

ACKNOWLEDGEMENTS

T hanks first to my family—my husband, Pete, my chief support as well as a talented editor, and my children, Danielle and Leo—for providing unwavering encouragement.

Unlike writers of fiction, nonfiction writers are not allowed to make things up. At every site where I searched for Henson, people supplied me with knowledge and data, pointed me to sources I might well have otherwise overlooked, and responded to my barrage of questions.

At La Grange (La Plata, Maryland) were Dr. Julia King, Michael J. Sullivan, Rebecca Webster, Janice Wilson, and Kevin Wilson.

At the Josiah Henson Special Park (Montgomery County, Maryland) were Keenan Holmes and Cassandra Michaud.

At Owensboro, Kentucky, were Leslie McCarty and Rich and Cindy Stierwalt.

And at Uncle Tom's Cabin Historic Site (Dresden, Ontario, Canada) were Barbara Carter, Steven Cook, Brenda Lambkin, and Lynda Weese.

Sonja Scharles accompanied me on this journey, taking photos, making contacts, reading and re-reading the manuscript, and generally serving as factotum.

Steven Cook, site manager at Uncle Tom's Cabin Historic Site in Dresden, Canada, provided difficult-to-find information, read portions of the manuscript for accuracy, and provided illustrations.

Valerie Nyce, senior photography coordinator, Community Relations Department at the College of Southern Maryland, provided support in securing and preparing illustrations.

And finally, without the enthusiastic support of Banks Smither, acquisitions editor at The History Press, this book would not have seen the light.

Chapter 1

CHARLES COUNTY, MARYLAND

LA GRANGE

Josiah Henson—fugitive from slavery, Underground Railroad hero, founder of a settlement and school for escaped slaves in Canada, and an inspiration for the character of Uncle Tom in the famous novel *Uncle Tom's Cabin*—was once an international celebrity. A household name in the nineteenth century in much of the eastern United States, Ontario, Canada, and London, England, Henson has largely disappeared from history. Until recently, most people in Charles County were unaware of this abolitionist hero, even though he was born near them at La Grange, a historic home in La Plata, Maryland.

When Kevin Wilson's late wife, Carey, drove past La Grange in 1989, she noticed a "For Sale" sign. Drawn to the beauty of the house and its surroundings, she contacted the owners, the La Hoods. Only after talking with the owners and a realtor did she approach her husband, Kevin, a carpenter and home builder who had grown up in an old farmhouse and had an appreciation for venerable historic structures. Like his wife, he found the house and the prospect of renovating it appealing, so the couple agreed to buy it. After nine months of renovations, the Wilsons moved into La Grange.

One of the largest surviving pre–Revolutionary War homes in Charles County, La Grange is situated on the western edge of the town of La Plata

La Grange. *Charles County Historical Society Photographs.*

about a mile and a half from historic Port Tobacco. Originally a Native American village named Potobac (named for the local tribe, not the crop), Port Tobacco was visited by Captain John Smith in 1608. With access to both the Chesapeake Bay and the Atlantic Ocean, Port Tobacco thrived and grew to become the first county seat.

Built by James Craik in 1765, La Grange is a two-story, gable-roofed frame house with brick ends and four exterior brick chimneys. The house is admired for its harmonious Georgian exterior, elegant interior, and pleasant surrounding lawns. The National Register Properties (Maryland Inventory CH-3) lauds La Grange for its "interesting coupling of the Georgian neoclassical style with an otherwise typical regional house plan" and ranks the house as "one of Maryland's most important historic and architectural landmarks."

Over the years, the house underwent major renovations. Francis Newman, who bought La Grange in 1798, added a full cellar, brick gable ends, and chimneys. After Nicholas Stonestreet bought the house in 1831, he switched the front entrance away from Port Tobacco toward what would become, decades later, the town of La Plata. Like in many early homes, the kitchen was detached from the main house to reduce the danger of fire. Stonestreet replaced the previous kitchen with a two-story brick kitchen that was later attached to the main house by a brick passageway.[1]

During his years at La Grange, Wilson said that the house provided him with an education in both architecture and history. He strived to make the house as authentic as possible, furnishing it with antiques appropriate to the style of the time. He also had a specialist analyze the exterior paint and had the house painted in its original straw-colored yellow.

Wilson also learned that in addition to being an architectural treasure, La Grange has links to regional and national history. Through speaking with previous owners George and Susan La Hood and J. Blacklock Wills, Wilson learned about his home's distinguished past.

JAMES CRAIK

In 1662, Henry Moore purchased a large parcel of land, then known as Mooreditch or Moore's Ditch, which included the land on which La Grange sits. Over the centuries, the land was re-divided and transferred to many other owners, the most famous being James Craik.

James Craik historical marker.
Photo by Sonja Scharles.

Born in Scotland in July 1730, James Craik had a long, illustrious career. He received medical training at Scotland's University of Edinburgh and, after graduation, joined the British army to provide medical service. He moved to the West Indies in 1751 to serve as an army surgeon but soon resigned and took up private practice in colonial Virginia, first in Norfolk and then Winchester. In 1754, Craik again joined the military, this time as a unit surgeon in the Virginia Provincial Regiment. During the French and Indian War, Craik became a close friend of George Washington's.

In 1756, James Craik retired from the army, bought a plantation at Port Tobacco and resumed his medical practice. However, on two occasions, he accompanied Washington on a trip to the Ohio River Valley to view lands awarded to Washington for his service during the French and Indian War. Although Craik built La Grange in 1765, within a decade he was involved in pre–Revolutionary War activities. Returning to the Continental army, he rose to the second-highest medical position. After the war, Craik served as Washington's personal physician. At Washington's urging, Craik moved to Alexandria, Virginia, and opened a medical practice. In 1796, La Grange became the property of his son, William Craik.

Craik was summoned to Mount Vernon on December 13, 1799; his friend and colleague George Washington was gravely ill. Craik, along with two other physicians, Dr. Gustavus R. Brown from Charles County and Dr. Elisha Cullen Dick of Alexandria, made every effort to save the former president, but Washington died the following day. Craik remained in Alexandria until his death in 1814.

Craik is well known nationwide among American historians and is a familiar name to Charles Countians; Dr. James Craik Elementary School is named after him, and along Route 6, at the entrance to La Grange, a historical marker reads, "Dr. James Craik, friend and family physician of Gen. Washington, built this place, La Grange, about 1765 and lived here until his removal to Alexandria, VA., 1783."

Craik died in 1814, when Josiah Henson would have been in his teens. These two men who lived at La Grange, so different in every aspect of their lives, nevertheless represent heroic American struggles for independence—Craik through serving in the Revolutionary War and Henson through struggling to free himself and his family from enslavement.

Francis Newman

While James Craik was La Grange's most famous owner, Francis Newman was certainly its most infamous. In the opening paragraphs of all four of his autobiographies, Henson states that he was born in Charles County, about one mile from Port Tobacco on the farm owned by Francis Newman,[2] the man to whom James Craik's son, William, sold La Grange on November 13, 1798.

Newman, born in England around 1759, married his first cousin Frances. Within a few years, he and Lydia Sheridan, a married woman, began an affair. In May 1785, Newman abandoned his wife in England and moved to France with Lydia (who used the alias "Naomi" while in France). He did, however, return to London that October to visit his wife one month before she gave birth to his child. A few years later, Francis and Lydia moved to America, presumably to avoid the scandal that dogged them but possibly also due to the French Revolution. Shortly after Lydia's death in 1796, Newman, although still married to Frances, married Elizabeth Friers. Newman originally bought a small tract of land and then added to it until he owned more than one thousand acres, including the site on which La Grange sits.

Before the War of 1812 broke out, Maryland governor Robert Bowie offered Newman the position of colonel of cavalry in the Maryland militia. Although Newman accepted the position, he realized that the property he owned in England would be confiscated if war broke out, so he accepted with the understanding that he would resign his commission immediately if war was declared—an act of self-preservation, but certainly not of patriotism.

In addition to being a bigamist, Newman defrauded the government. As Jean B. Lee explained in *The Price of Nationhood: The American Revolution in Charles County*, a deep economic depression gripped Charles County after the Revolutionary War, and several insolvent planters amassed large tax debts.[3] Newman, appointed tax collector by 1814, may have been unable to collect taxes; on the other hand, he may have collected the taxes and fraudulently failed to turn them into the government.

Newman's own debts grew so large that the United States Treasury Department scheduled a marshal's sale of all his Charles County property, including La Grange, for January 16, 1818. Whether the sale ever took place is unknown. The year after Newman made his will, he added a codicil instructing Friers to sell La Grange to Wilfred Manning, as he had previously arranged, and then to sell the rest of his property in Charles County—which would have included the enslaved—to help pay off his debts.[4]

The enslaved at La Grange would neither have known nor cared about issues of bigamy, patriotism, and tax fraud. For them, the issue was more personal: Newman was a cruel master.

Josiah McPherson

Josiah's mother, three sisters, and two brothers lived on Francis Newman's farm, but Newman was not their slaveholder. Henson's father was enslaved by Newman, and although Josiah was born at La Grange, Josiah, his mother, and his siblings were enslaved by Dr. Josiah McPherson, who hired their mother out to work for Newman, a common practice among slaveholders.

The location of McPherson's estate in Charles County has not yet been identified. Michael Sullivan, a Charles County businessman and avid historian, posited that the estate the Henson family referred to belonged not to Dr. McPherson but to McPherson's sister, a distinction that young Josiah would not have recognized. It's also feasible that McPherson and his wife may have lived in Charles County with one of her relatives while he practiced medicine in nearby Montgomery County.

Several records, including the 1800 United States Census, place McPherson in Montgomery County. An 1801 act of the Maryland Assembly lists McPherson as one of four men charged with laying out the town of Rockville, and a subsequent supplement to the act in 1803 names him as one of three men appointed to administer the town's survey.

In the *Autobiography of Josiah Henson, an Inspiration for Harriet Beecher Stowe's Uncle Tom*, Henson wrote that McPherson was "was far kinder to his slaves than the planters generally were, never suffering them to be struck by any one. He was a man of good, kind impulses, liberal, jovial, hearty."[5]

McPherson was obviously fond of the young Henson: he named him Josiah after himself and added the name Henson for one of his uncles who was an officer in the Revolutionary War. Henson described his time on McPherson's estate as "a bright spot in [his] childhood."

That bright spot was soon obliterated. Henson said that although McPherson "maintained a high reputation for goodness of heart and an almost saint-like benevolence, the habit of intemperance steadily gained ground, and finally occasioned his death."[6] McPherson was found one morning, drowned in a stream less than a foot deep. He had returned from a party, presumably fallen from his horse and was too drunk to save himself.

After Josiah McPherson died, his property had to be sold to pay his debts, with the remaining assets to be divided among his heirs. The inventory of his property included medical books and devices, confirming Henson's statement that McPherson was a doctor. It also included an inventory of enslaved workers dated June 1805 that lists a nine-year-old boy named Sye, described as infirm, for sale for thirty dollars. Although Josiah never described himself as infirm in his childhood, he said he was often called Sie or Siah, and since he clearly stated that he and his family were enslaved by McPherson, the boy listed in the inventory is almost certainly Josiah. Since Josiah said that he and his mother were sold at the same auction, the woman

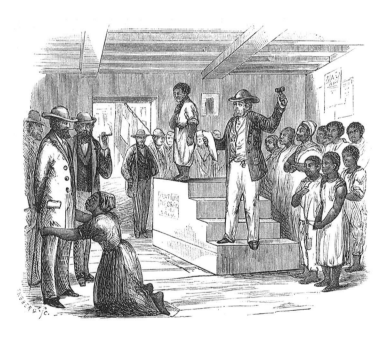

Auction of an enslaved child. *New York Public Library.*

19

named Celia, age fifty, listed on the inventory is probably his mother. A boy named John, age twelve, is also on the inventory. In later years, Henson bought the freedom of his brother John, enslaved in Maryland, who may well have been the child indicated on the 1805 inventory.

Josiah listed the terrors the enslaved community felt at the upcoming auction: "The first sad announcement that the sale was to be; the knowledge that all ties of the past were to be sundered; the frantic terror at the idea of being sent 'down south'; the almost certainty that one member of a family will be torn from another; the anxious scanning of purchasers' faces; the agony of parting, often for ever, with husband, wife, child—these must be seen and felt to be fully understood."[7]

Henson lived on McPherson's estate for only two or three years. Young as he was, Henson said that he maintained a photographic memory of every detail of the day the enslaved were auctioned off. At the Rockville auction, his brothers and sisters were sold first. Then his mother was bought by Isaac Riley of Montgomery County. When Josiah was put on the auction block, his mother pushed through the crowd and begged Riley to buy him too, but his response was to hit and kick her until she retreated. Josiah was sold to Adam Robb of Montgomery County.

Digging for Henson

Henson, who by the late 1800s was probably as famous as Craik had been, had faded from history to the extent that Kevin Wilson, prior to receiving a request for an archaeological dig on his property in the spring of 2016, was unfamiliar with the name Josiah Henson and the fact that this once famous man might have been born at La Grange.

Michael Sullivan, however, did know a great deal about Henson. An avid historian since his teenage years, Sullivan came across this passage in 1958 when he read the newly published *The History of Charles County Maryland, Written on Its Tercentenary Year of 1958*: "Early in the 19th century there lived in Charles County a negro slave named Josiah Henson. His early life was of such hardship that he finally escaped to Canada in 1830, where he became a Methodist minister. Harriet Beecher Stowe used the story of Josiah Henson's slave life as the basis for her character of Uncle Tom in the famous book 'Uncle Tom's Cabin,' which was such a powerful influence in bringing an end to slavery in the United States."[8] This brief description whetted

Left: Michael Sullivan. *Photo by Sonja Scharles.*

Right: Julia King. *Photo by Cody L. Dorsey.*

Sullivan's interest, and over the years, he continued to read about Henson and research his life. His goal became finding Henson's birthplace.

In his autobiographies, Henson wrote that he "was born June 15, 1789, in Charles county, Maryland, on a farm belonging to Mr. Francis Newman, about a mile from Port Tobacco." However, that birthdate cannot be accurate. In 1794, Newman had not yet emigrated from England to America. Newman didn't buy La Grange until 1798, nearly nine years after the year Henson claims as his birthdate.

The issue of Henson's birthdate is further complicated by the 1805 sales inventory, which lists a nine-year-old boy named Sye. If Henson was nine in 1805, he would have been born in 1796. Since McPherson was Henson's slaveholder and was personally fond of him, he would likely have known his age. The Uncle Tom's Cabin Historic Site in Dresden, Ontario, accepts 1796 as the probable birthdate. However, 1796 predates Newman's purchase of the land by two years.

Henson's manumission papers (the documents certifying that a person is free) lists his age as thirty in March 1829, which would make his date of birth 1798. It is possible that the 1789 birthdate in his autobiographies could have been a simple error, transposing the last two numbers, turning 1798 into 1789. Since the year 1789 appears in all four autobiographies, it's conceivable that the original error was simply copied in subsequent works.

Many enslaved persons did not know their birthdates. Sales inventories, since they may be based on missing or incorrect data, can also contain errors. Even Henson's manumission document, if based on incorrect information, could be in error. Although it's impossible to say with certainty when Henson was born, the date of 1789 is clearly incorrect. It is likely, however, that he was born at La Grange.

To locate the site of Henson's birth, Sullivan enlisted the help of Dr. Julia King, professor of anthropology at St. Mary's College of Maryland. King had previously collaborated with Sullivan to discover the original Charles County Courthouse and Zekiah Fort. Funding for the La Grange archaeological project was provided by L. Gordon Croft, a Baltimore businessman born in Charles County.

Under the direction of Dr. King, a crew of six current students and recent graduates of St. Mary's College of Maryland worked during May and June 2016. The assistant project archaeologist, Rebecca Webster, was in charge of the daily activities in the field and the lab. The crew was aided for one week by two high school interns sponsored by the Charles County NAACP.[9]

King realized that finding concrete evidence of Henson's birth would clearly be impossible; as she quipped to *Washington Post* reporter Joe Heim, "We're not going to find a piece of ceramic that says 'Josiah Henson was born here'"[10] Historian Jean B. Lee pointed out that little documentary evidence exists for enslaved persons in the Chesapeake area beyond aggregate numbers in census and tax records and sales or estate inventories that list names, gender, and age.[11] Even the sparse documentation that exists may be compromised since dates might be mere estimates and names might be changed by a new slaveholder.

To find archaeological evidence of Henson's birthplace, the crew searched for evidence of slave quarters or other outbuildings that could have been used to house the enslaved workers. The record of their archaeological excavation, *In Search of Josiah Henson's Birthplace*, includes a discussion of the placement of slave quarters on plantations. While some plantation owners preferred to build quarters in view of the main house, making ongoing surveillance possible, others preferred to keep the quarters out of sight. In Charles County, the placement of slave quarters varied, but "hiding quarters, or at least placing them in marginal locations appears to have been a relatively common practice in late-18th- and 19th-century Charles County."[12]

Although plantation owners wouldn't situate quarters on soil better suited to growing profitable crops, they might place the quarters for fieldworkers close to those fields. When the crew discovered an area where

Rebecca Webster. *Photo by Julia King.*

the soil was unsuited for agriculture because it was predominately clay and would flood easily, they knew that this would be a likely site for the quarters. The discovery of the quarters' location came through bricks: the crew discovered four concentrations of bricks, which they believe to have been chimneys for wooden structures. The accumulation of evidence of slave quarters, King said, is more than enough to make the case that Henson was probably born at La Grange.[13]

Webster said that the crew found artifacts—including ceramics, nails, glass, buttons, tobacco pipes, and even fish scales—in a field near La Grange. More artifacts were found nearer the house than at a distance, but Webster explained that because the enslaved owned fewer possessions, the distribution is consistent with many other archaeological searches.

In speaking about the excavation, Webster said that, for her, the most interesting discoveries are those that provide insights into the lives of the enslaved. For example, fish scales may indicate "activities that the enslaved community might have partaken in. While the master did provide some food for slaves, the slaves kept their own gardens, some raised chickens, and if there was a water source nearby, they could go fishing." La Grange, she pointed out, offers several nearby waterways suitable for fishing.

Webster noted that a button and buckle found in the area around the quarters also rank among the most noteworthy artifacts for her. Although a buckle might seem more likely to belong to a house slave than to a fieldworker, "archaeological and historical research has demonstrated that slaves created a local economy where they might sell the produce from their gardens, eggs

Janice Wilson. *Photo by Janice Wilson.*

from their chickens, or perform odd jobs in exchange for money. With that money, they would go out and buy various items, including items of personal adornment. These items allowed for them to express their individuality in a system that tried to take that away."

Kevin Wilson said that owning a historic home requires a lot of TLC—time, labor, and cash. In January 2017, he reluctantly decided to sell the house. On March 25, 2017, Michael Sullivan, Julia King, and Janice Wilson, president of the Charles County NAACP, spoke to the Southern Maryland Delegation of the Maryland General Assembly about Josiah Henson, his connection to La Grange, and its historical significance to Maryland. The delegation enthusiastically agreed to allot $980,000 for the purchase of La Grange.

The Maryland General Assembly appointed the College of Southern Maryland to hold the funds to purchase the property until the entity that takes over the management of the property has been identified. It also appointed a committee of stakeholders—the Charles County NAACP, St. Mary's College of Maryland, the College of Southern Maryland, and the Charles County government—to recommend the best use of the property. A historic marker will be added to that of James Craik on the property, but plans for turning La Grange into an African American tourist site similar to those of Frederick Douglass, Harriet Tubman, and Thurgood Marshall have not yet been developed. Options include creating a museum to Henson at La Grange, restoring the house and land to resemble the original plantation, and coordinating with the National Park Service to connect La Grange with the nearby Thomas Stone House, a National Historic Site.

La Grange, the home of both Craik and Henson, is located a mere mile and a half from Haberdeventure, better known as the Thomas Stone House. Stone, one of the fifty-six signers of the Declaration of Independence, was a lawyer and a slaveholding planter. He died in 1787, about a decade before the birth of Josiah Henson. Within a few decades in this small geographical area, Craik fought in the Revolutionary War, Stone signed the Declaration of Independence, and Henson waged his own battle for freedom from tyranny.

When the 2016 dig at La Grange began, most Charles Countians had not heard of Josiah Henson. Since then, newspaper and magazine articles have focused on him and his birthplace. Public lectures, town hall meetings, and events, many spearheaded by Janice Wilson, have made Henson, if not yet a household name, familiar to many in the region.

Life at La Grange

Henson's experiences at La Grange illustrate many of slavery's atrocities. Being so young, Henson had few memories of his life at La Grange; however, one incident remained vivid. Josiah's father, hearing his wife's screams, ran to her aid and discovered that the overseer had attacked and possibly raped her—a not uncommon barbarity. Henson said, "My father sprang upon him like a tiger. In a moment the overseer was down, and, mastered by rage, my father would have killed him but for the entreaties of my mother."[14] Although the overseer said he wouldn't tell anyone of the incident, he broke his promise.

In slave states, laws allowed cruel punishments for any enslaved person striking a white person, regardless of the circumstances. The punishment for Henson's father was to have his right ear nailed to a whipping post, receive one hundred lashes, and then have his ear severed. Henson said that the crowd witnessing the event cheered.

Henson noted that his father abruptly changed after the punishment. Before, he had been "a good-humored and light-hearted man, the ringleader in all fun at corn-huskings and Christmas buffoonery. His banjo was the life of the farm, and all night long at a merry-making would he play on it while the other negroes danced."[15] After being beaten and maimed, Henson's father became morose, surly, and bitter. Like many enslaved persons deemed potentially threatening or uncompliant, Henson's father was sold to the Deep South.

The slave states loosely comprised two regions. Although definitions vary, the Upper South is generally considered to include states closer to the northern abolitionist states, including Arkansas, North Carolina, Tennessee, Maryland, and Virginia, while the Lower or Deep South included Alabama, Georgia, Mississippi, South Carolina, Louisiana, and Florida. Although slavery was an atrocity in every region, there were distinctions. Being sold to the Deep South was, for the slaveholder, a way of getting rid of an unwanted slave. For the enslaved in the Deep South, work was harder, punishments crueler, provisions more meager, diseases more common, escape more difficult, and mortality rates far higher than in the Upper South.

When Dr. Josiah McPherson, the slaveholder of the Henson family, learned that Henson's father had been beaten, mutilated, and sold, he refused to hire his enslaved out to Newman again. Henson's mother and siblings returned to McPherson's estate in Charles County. Henson noted that Newman sold Henson's father to a son in Alabama, and Josiah and his mother never heard from him again. However, Newman's only son had a plantation in Louisiana, so that was probably Henson's father's destination.[16]

Chapter 2

MONTGOMERY COUNTY, MARYLAND

ADAM ROBB

After being sold to Adam Robb at the Rockville auction, presumably for around the thirty dollars listed in the McPherson sales inventory, Henson was moved about forty miles north of Charles County to the town of Rockville in Montgomery County, Maryland. Still a young child, probably between seven and nine years old, Henson found himself separated from his mother and siblings for the first time.

Robb, a prominent Rockville citizen, owned Robb's Tavern. Because he rented horses and carriages to customers for travel to nearby towns, the tavern served as a popular overnight stop. The tavern also served as a site for public sales and auctions.

Henson found himself housed on one of Robb's farms in overcrowded quarters with about forty others. Robb's treatment of his enslaved workers was brutal, and they were too demoralized to care for a new child thrust among them, although Henson said that someone would occasionally give him a piece of corn bread or salted herring. Henson, labeled by McPherson in the sales inventory as infirm, became increasingly feeble. Eventually, he noted, he "lay for some days almost dead on the ground."[17]

This bleak stage of his life, however, was brief. Robb encountered Isaac Riley, who had purchased Henson's mother at the auction, and offered to sell Josiah to him. Because both men realized that young Henson was gravely ill and might not survive, he was of little value to either man. Nevertheless, they struck a deal: Riley would take Henson. If Henson died, he would pay Robb nothing; if Henson lived, Riley, a blacksmith, would do a little horseshoeing for Robb.

Henson described it as a "blessed change," saying, "I had been lying on a lot of rags, thrown on a dirt floor. All day long I had been left alone, crying for water, crying for mother; the slaves, who left at daylight, when they returned cared nothing for me." Now he was reunited with his mother, whom he called his "best friend on earth."[18]

Life on Isaac Riley's Plantation

Moving to the Riley plantation marked a turning point in Henson's life. The child, once so weak he could barely move, began to thrive and show signs of the man he would become. Despite his joy at being reunited with his mother, he later described Isaac Riley to his friend Henry Bleby as "coarse and vulgar in his habits, profligate, unprincipled, and cruel."[19]

His description of life on the Riley plantation provides a window into the lives of enslaved fieldworkers on plantations. His first chores, he said, were carrying pails of water for the workers and holding the horse plow to weed between corn rows. He added, "As I grew older and taller, I was entrusted with the care of master's saddle-horse." He then became old enough to work all day in the fields and said that "it was not long before I could do it, at least as well as my associates in misery."[20] This brief description of his increasing work responsibilities highlights two dominant traits that remain apparent throughout his life: his competitiveness and the value he assigned to others' trust in and admiration for him.

Henson's depiction of enslaved life on a plantation resembles that of Frederick Douglass, who was also enslaved in Maryland. Born in Talbot County, Maryland, circa 1819, Douglass escaped from slavery in 1838, eight years after Henson. Douglass's descriptions of plantation life in his 1845 autobiography, *Narrative of the Life of Frederick Douglass, an American Slave*, echo those in Henson's narrative.

For sustenance, Henson said the enslaved workers were provided with cornmeal, salted herring and, in summer, a little buttermilk. The workers were also granted a small patch of land on which to grow vegetables to augment their diet. During most of the year, they had two daily meals:

breakfast at noon, when they broke from the work that began at dawn, and supper when the day's work concluded. In harvest season, when the workload was even heavier because they had to bring crops in quickly, workers received three meals.

Douglass also described the inadequacy of the food. The monthly allotment consisted of eight pounds of pork or fish—roughly a little more than four ounces a day—and one bushel of cornmeal. In both Douglass's and Henson's descriptions, the amount of food provided was clearly inadequate for people doing grueling fieldwork from sunup to sundown.

Because of a scarcity of food, enslaved workers had to grow as much food as possible on small patches of land, fish if streams were nearby, forage for berries or other edible food, hunt for game, make occasional nighttime raids on orchards, and use every opportunity to provide themselves with food.

Douglass said that the orchard on the plantation of Colonel Lloyd north of Easton in Talbot County was "a temptation to the hungry swarms of boys, as well as the older slaves, belonging to the colonel, few of whom had the virtue or the vice to resist it."[21] The penalty for stealing a piece of fruit was harsh, and Douglass said that almost every day in the summer, someone received a lashing. To prevent the loss of fruit, the colonel finally had the fence surrounding the orchard covered with tar, and any enslaved persons found with tar on them received a severe lashing.

Henson helped relieve the relentless hunger by occasionally stealing a chicken or driving a sheep or pig into the woods, slaughtering it, and surreptitiously sharing it with the enslaved "for the good of those whom Riley was starving." He described these acts in terms of chivalry: "No white knight, rescuing a *white* fair lady from cruel oppression, ever felt the throbbing of a chivalrous heart more intensely than I, a *black* knight, did, when running down a chicken to hide it in an out-of-the-way place till dark, that I might be able then to carry it to some poor overworked fair black one, to whom it was at once food, luxury, and medicine….I felt good, moral, heroic."[22] Later, when he was in charge of the farm's crops and selling them at market, he diverted some of the money earned from market sales to supply food for the hungry workers. These desperate attempts of the enslaved to relieve their hunger fueled the notion among slaveholders that the enslaved were untrustworthy and prone to stealing, arguments they frequently used against the abolitionist cause.

Clothing on the Riley plantation mirrored that of most plantations: Henson said that children were provided only a shirt of tow cloth, a coarse, heavy linen. Older girls were provided one dress, and older boys were given crude trousers to wear with the shirt. Workers received one pair of shoes each year, and in the winter in colder climates, they were given a jacket or coat and a hat.

In his narrative, Frederick Douglass pointed out that "children unable to work in the field had neither shoes, stockings, jackets, nor trousers, given to them; their clothing consisted of two coarse linen shirts per year. When these failed them, they went naked until the next allowance-day."[23]

In addition to a scarcity of food and inadequate clothing, the lodging for enslaved laborers was appalling. Henson described the dirt-floored log huts:

> *In a single room were huddled, like cattle, ten or a dozen persons, men, women, and children. All ideas of refinement and decency were, of course, out of the question. We had neither bedsteads, nor furniture of any description. Our beds were collections of straw and old rags, thrown down in the corners and boxed in with boards; a single blanket the only covering....The wind whistled and the rain and snow blew in through the cracks, and the damp earth soaked in the moisture till the floor was miry as a pig-sty. Such were our houses. In these wretched hovels were we penned at night, and fed by day; here were the children born and the sick—neglected.*[24]

A slave cabin. *Wikimedia Commons.*

Douglass also stated that the enslaved slept on a dirt floor with only one blanket, but he added another dimension to his description of plantation life, saying that they suffered more from the lack of time to sleep than from the lack of a bed. After their work in the field was done, Douglass explained, they had their "washing, mending, and cooking to do, and having few or none of the ordinary facilities for doing either of these, very many of their sleeping hours are consumed in preparing for the field the coming day; and when this is done, old and young, male and female, married and single drop down side by side, on one common bed—the cold, damp floor."[25]

Despite the heavy work, the paucity of food, and the deplorable living conditions, Henson thrived. By age fifteen, he said, "I could run faster, wrestle better, and jump higher than anybody about me." Henson described his growing competitiveness and self-esteem:

> All this caused my master and my fellow-slaves to look upon me as a wonderfully smart fellow, and prophecy the great things I should do when I became a man. My vanity became vastly inflamed, and I fully coincided in their opinion. Julius Caesar never aspired and plotted for the imperial crown more ambitiously than did I to out-hoe, out-reap, out-husk, out-dance, out-strip every competitor; and from all I can learn he never enjoyed his triumph half as much. One word of commendation from the petty despot who ruled over us would set me up for a month.[26]

After Henson caught Isaac Riley's overseer stealing from his employer, Riley fired the overseer, and Henson took his place as superintendent in charge of farm work, where he says he was able to "double the crops with more cheerful and willing labour, than was ever seen on the estate before."[27] He was in charge not only of the care of all the crops but also of taking them to market and selling them.

Although most overseers were white, there were exceptions. Using an enslaved worker as overseer saved the plantation owner the salary he would have paid a white overseer, while also maintaining more control over the enslaved overseer than he would have had over a free man. However, Henson's usual reward for his work, he reported, was being cursed for not getting higher prices at the markets, adding, "My master was a fearful blasphemer. Clearly as he saw my profitableness to him, he was too much of a brute to reward me with kindness or even decent treatment."[28]

One of the many skills that Henson developed and put to good use throughout his life was what he termed "connivance," a word with a negative connotation that implies being secretively involved in some sort of plot. This was also a term frequently used by proslavery advocates. Because the enslaved were "conniving," they argued, they could not be trusted and should not be in a free society. But connivance, sometimes in the guise of subterfuge and sometimes in acts of innovation, allowed enslaved people to cope with difficult and dangerous situations. One of the most famous examples is when Harriet Tubman eluded slave catchers who were closing in on her. Overhearing some men read a wanted poster that said she was illiterate, she simply opened a book and pretended to be reading it intently; the men glanced at her and moved on.

Isaac Riley, at age forty-five, married Matilda, an eighteen-year-old "who had some little property, and more thrift." Matilda often complained that Henson had not gotten the best prices for the products he sold at the markets. He knew she was timid, uneducated, and superstitious. When he overheard her complaining to Isaac, the next morning Henson would, from a distance but close enough for Matilda to see him, speak to a small ball to which he had attached a thread. As he talked to the ball, it would bounce up and down, the string invisible at a distance. Henson recounted an incident in which he said, "'So, Missis Riley thinks I didn't get enough for her butter'? Up would come the ball. 'I got all it was worth?' Down the little ball would go. It was astonishing what a reputation for cleverness that ball obtained in my hands. 'Why it knows everything,' I once heard my mistress say."[29]

Like most of the enslaved, Henson was illiterate. He had made his first attempt to learn to read when he was about thirteen. A boy named William, enslaved by Lewis Bell, drove Bell's sons back and forth to school daily. William listened to the children as they talked about their lessons and learned to read and write. When Henson heard William read, he was eager to learn too. William told him if he could buy a Webster's spelling book at a Washington store, William would teach him to read. In his eagerness, Henson made ink from charcoal and fashioned a pen out of a goose quill. He learned that *I* and *R*, the letters on the butter he sold in the markets, stood for "Isaac Riley," so those were the first letters he learned to write. By picking up apples that fell from the trees and selling them in the markets, he managed to get the eleven cents he needed and purchased the book.

Possessing books, newspapers, or other written material was dangerous for slaves, so like many slaves with written material, he hid the book inside his hat. The next morning, while harnessing a horse for Riley, the horse bolted, and as Henson ran to catch it, his hat fell to the ground, exposing the book. After Henson had captured the horse, Riley confronted him. Henson admitted that he had bought the book with money from selling apples in the orchard. In his fury, Riley beat the boy on his head and shoulders with his cane until he was unconscious. Henson was unable to work until he recovered, but when he saw Riley again, Riley said if he ever caught Henson with a book again, he would "knock [his] brains out." Lewis Bell, fearing that William might teach his other slaves to read, sold him to Georgia before anyone else could be "spoiled by that rascal." Henson would not attempt to learn to read again for more than four decades, and before then, his inability to read would enable Riley to defraud him out of his money and his freedom.

Without any instruction, Henson learned to do enough math to function well in his role in the markets in Washington, D.C., and Georgetown. He could obviously do basic addition and subtraction in order to handle money, and he said he was able to make accurate estimates and compute fractions.

In addition to learning basic math, Henson learned other valuable skills. He says he was "anxious to imitate those whom [he] respected as gentlemen," so he listened carefully to well-spoken people he encountered in the marketplaces of Maryland and Washington, D.C., and memorized phrases and sentences so that he could learn to speak well.[30] He also listened carefully to lawyers talk about their cases and developed a basic knowledge of law that he would later put to good use in Canada. The understanding of law that he absorbed through listening enabled him on several occasions to protect both his own rights and those of others.

Henson's new position as overseer, he admitted, increased his pride and his ambition. Many of the traits he exhibited—loyalty, ambition, hard work, and dependability—made him widely admired and praised. But ironically, as decades passed and the abolitionist cause advanced, the traits that once won him praise caused him to be dismissed or mocked as servile and obsequious.

Two life-altering events—one spiritual, one physical—occurred during his time on the Riley plantation. Henson described his mother as a devoutly Christian woman, given to frequent prayers. When he was eighteen, she told him to ask Riley's permission to hear John McKenny preach at Newport Mill, located nearby on the bank of Rock Creek. McKenny, a baker by trade, was an inspiring preacher who lived only a few miles from the Riley plantation. As an abolitionist, McKenny refused to hire the enslaved to work in his bakery since their wages would be paid to their slaveholders.

Despite his mother's urgings, Henson was at first reluctant to approach Riley because he had often been beaten for making similar requests, but finally he asked Riley for permission to go. He couldn't answer Riley's questions about why he wanted to go or what good it would do him and admitted it was his mother's idea. After assuring Riley that he would return immediately after the meeting, Henson got permission to go.

Up to this point, Henson said, he had never heard a sermon or any conversations about religion except from his mother. When he was little, his mother taught him the Lord's Prayer, and he had frequently heard her pray. She had also stressed to him since childhood that everyone is responsible to a supreme being.

As a black man, Henson wasn't allowed into the meetinghouse, but he managed to see McKenny through the open door and hear him preach. The text of the sermon was Hebrews 2:9: "But we see Jesus, who was made a little lower than the angels for the suffering of death, crowned with glory and honour; that he by the grace of God should taste death for every man." It was the "for every man" McKenny emphasized, saying that Christ died "for the high, for the low, for the rich, for the poor, for the bond, the free, the negro in his chains, the man in gold and diamonds."[31] For the first time, Henson realized that in the eyes of God, the enslaved were equal to the slaveholders and that Jesus's death redeemed him personally, as well as those who oppressed him. This text from Hebrews was the first Bible verse that Henson had ever heard, and he says that he recalled it almost every day of his life.

Henson's conversion was a pivotal experience because his new religious beliefs shaped key decisions he made throughout his life. Religion also became his vocation. He spoke of the gospel to the enslaved workers on the Riley plantation and began to pray with them. His religious fervor continued, his preaching became widely admired, and by the second edition of his autobiography, he was referring to himself as Father Henson, a title by which many would come to know him.

A year or two later, when he was nineteen or twenty, the second life-altering event occurred. Henson's first slaveholder, Dr. McPherson, died after falling off his horse when he returned home after drinking. What might seem an unusual death seems less so when considering Henson's descriptions of the recreational life common to plantation owners. Speaking of Riley, he said, "My master's habits were such as were common enough among the dissipated planters of the neighborhood; and one of their frequent practices was to assemble on Saturday or Sunday, which were their holidays, and gamble, run horses, or fight game-cocks, discuss politics, and drink whiskey and brandy-and-water all day long. Perfectly aware that they would not be able to find their own way home at night, each one ordered his body-servant to come after him and help him home."[32]

Seeing Riley safely home was one of Henson's duties, and he said that he frequently held Riley on his horse when he was too drunk to remain in the saddle. Not surprisingly, fights among the planters frequently broke out, and an additional duty was to disengage one's slaveholder from the fight and see him safely home. Henson's competitive nature and pride are evident in this task: "I knew that I was doing for him what he could not do for himself, showing my superiority to others, and acquiring their respect in some degree at the same time."[33]

Ongoing tensions existed in the Riley family, and one night, Isaac Riley got into a fight with his brother George's overseer, Bryce Litton. Everyone there sided with Litton, and Riley called on Henson to help him. Henson said Riley was "crazy with drink and rage," and Henson struggled to get him out of the room, into the carriage and home.

During the fight, Litton had fallen. Henson said he doesn't know if Litton fell because he was drunk or if he had accidentally shoved him during the melee. But the cause was irrelevant—Litton was a white man who accused a black man of striking him. About one week later, on an errand to deliver some letters, Henson rode a horse down a lane that passed through the part of the farm owned by Isaac's brother George. On his return, Henson was ambushed by Litton and three of his enslaved workers. Henson was told to dismount from his horse, and at Litton's first violent blow with a stick, the horse ran away, leaving Henson no means of escape.

When Henson continued trying to defend himself, Litton became enraged and attacked him with a fence post. Henson describes the beating: "The ponderous blow fell; I lifted my arm to ward it off, the bone cracked like a pipe-stem, and I fell headlong to the ground. Repeated blows then rained on my back till both shoulder-blades were broken, and the blood gushed copiously from my mouth."[34] When Litton finally stopped, he reminded Henson that the beating resulted from hitting a white man.

Riley was furious and lodged a complaint against Litton at the Montgomery County Courthouse, but Litton claimed that Henson had "sassed" him, jumped off his horse, and attacked him. Because no black man could testify against a white man, Litton was acquitted.

On the Riley plantation, no doctor was ever called to help the ill or injured enslaved people. Riley's sister, Miss Patty, put splints on Henson's arms and bound up his back. After five months, he returned to fieldwork. Although he regained strength and was able to do much of the farm work, his arms and shoulders were permanently damaged.

Reverend Henry Bleby, a missionary from the West Indies, first encountered Henson in Boston in July 1858 at a weekly meeting of ministers. Bleby's first impression upon noticing Henson was that he seemed a good-natured, fun-loving man. After being introduced to Henson, Bleby immediately noted that Henson's arms were badly crippled. Bleby said that Henson's arms appeared to be disproportionally short and stiff, and because of the damage to his shoulders, when he needed to put on or remove his hat, he needed to lower his head to his hands. The damage was so apparent that when Bleby published a biography of Henson in 1873, he titled it *Josiah: The Maimed Fugitive.*

Unlike his father, who had become bitter and morose, Henson managed to put aside anger and devote himself to his farm work. Motivated partly by pride and partly by what he considered his Christian values of duty and forgiveness, Henson continued his position as overseer, acknowledging that Riley was pleased by saving the salary of a white overseer.

Henson said that he gradually became responsible for selling everything raised or produced on the farm and that he negotiated better prices than anyone else Riley could have entrusted. The farm grew tobacco, potatoes, corn, barley, wheat, and oats and produced hay, fruit, and butter. Livestock included cattle, pigs, chickens, and sheep. The size of the farms that Henson oversaw varied from year to year. Some of the tracts farmed may have belonged to other Riley family members. Also, as debts mounted in lean years, some parcels on the edge of the property were undoubtedly sold to clear debts; in good years, outlying parcels would have been purchased to expand the plantation's acreage.

Henson also noted that he gained and maintained his position as overseer because Riley was "quite incompetent to attend to the business himself." He summed up the interplay of pride and Christian values in his position:

> *For many years I was his factotum, and supplied him with all his means for all his purposes, whether they were good or bad. I had no reason to think highly of his moral character; but it was my duty to be faithful to him in the position in which he placed me; and I can boldly declare, before God and man, that I was so. I forgave him the careless blows and injuries he had inflicted on me in my childhood and youth, and was proud of the favour he now showed me, and of the character and reputation I had earned by strenuous and persevering efforts.* [35]

During this period of relative security, when he was twenty-two, Henson married Charlotte, who was enslaved at Williamsburg, a nearby plantation. No record of the Hensons' marriage exists, but marriages between slaves usually amounted to some type of ceremony, such as "jumping the broomstick," in which the slaveholder would hold a broomstick across the cabin doorway and the couple would jump across it. Such marriages, however, were not legal arrangements, and if a minister were present, he might conclude the ceremony by saying that the marriage would last until circumstances, distance, or death separated the couple. When couples were separated through auction, sales, or transfers to another plantation by the same slaveholder, the slaveholder often encouraged or even demanded that the individuals remarry—especially if the women were of childbearing age.

Henson's choice of Charlotte as a wife reflects his values: he described her as well taught, efficient, pious, and kind. Looking back on the years, he said she had given him twelve children, seven of whom survived. By the end of his life, that number would be reduced to six. The prospect of losing six of twelve children is horrifying today, but in the nineteenth century, losing enslaved children through disease, injury, or accident was not uncommon, nor was losing them through private sales or auctions.

Although Henson was enslaved to Isaac Riley until he and his family escaped to Canada, he was unable to remain in Montgomery County. The next stop on his odyssey would be Kentucky. He would return to the Riley house twice more in his life—once when he had been living in Kentucky but was still enslaved by Isaac and once years later when he was a free man living in Canada.

THE RILEY/BOLTON HOUSE

The term *plantation* evokes for most people a grand house on a huge estate, like Tara in *Gone with the Wind* or one of the surviving historic antebellum homes. But the word *plantation* more aptly describes a farm where crops are planted, and Isaac Riley's house was just that—a farmhouse, not a mansion.

The Riley house, located on 11420 Old Georgetown Road in North Bethesda, is a two-story frame building with an attached log wing. The farmhouse, built prior to the log wing, was probably built by either William

The Riley/Bolton House. *Montgomery County Parks*.

Collyer or Isaac Riley's older brother, George, to whom Collyer's son, James, had sold the property sometime between 1790 and 1815, the year of George Riley's death.

The log section, one room with a fireplace and exterior chimney, was added by Matilda Riley shortly after her husband Isaac's death in 1850. The *Historical Structure Report* prepared for the site by John Milner Associates in 2008 noted that the log wing may have originally been built as an outbuilding and served as a kitchen where enslaved workers prepared meals. It's unclear if the log room was originally separate from the house and later moved and attached to it or if the two sections were always connected. The passageway connecting the house to the log wing wasn't added until the renovations in the 1930s. Prior to adding the passageway, assuming that the room was used as a kitchen, prepared meals may have been taken out of the log room and brought to the door of the house for the family's meals and also handed out the log room door to workers returning from the fields for their meals.

Like most historic homes, the Riley/Bolton House passed through a succession of owners. The *Historic Structure Report* lists William Collyer as the first owner of the house and his son, James Collyer, as the second. George Riley, the older brother of Isaac, became the third owner.[36]

After George Riley's first wife died, he married Mary Richards. When George died in 1815, Isaac Riley was living in the house and remained there for the rest of his life. George's widow, Mary Riley, married Arnold Thomas Windsor in 1818.

Relations between Windsor and Isaac Riley were always contentious. Windsor was now the husband of Isaac Riley's sister-in-law, Mary Riley Windsor. Windsor filed several lawsuits against Riley, accusing him of mismanagement of the farm. The goal of the suits was to force Riley to sell parcels of land previously owned by George, his wife's former husband. In discussing his role on the farm, Henson claimed that he held his management position because of Riley's incompetence, so Windsor's accusations may have had merit. In response to Windsor's lawsuits, Riley began to file countersuits. The suits dragged on for years, and Riley's financial situation became increasingly dire; in 1825, he felt he might lose everything. Riley's solution, which he deemed temporary, was to send his enslaved workers to his brother's plantation in Kentucky so they couldn't be seized by the sheriff and auctioned off to pay his debts.

Accompanying the stereotypical image of plantations as having large, elegant mansions is the assumption of wealth and the lifestyle it provides. But La Grange, where Henson was born, was sold to clear debts after Francis Newman died. Henson was sold to pay debts after Josiah McPherson died, and then he and all the enslaved workers on the Riley plantation would also have been sold to settle Isaac Riley's debts. For plantation owners, the enslaved provided not just labor—they also served as liquid assets.

When Isaac Riley died in 1850, his wife, Matilda, inherited the estate, and upon her death in 1890, her daughter, Frances Ruben Riley Mace, inherited the property. The house remained in the Riley family for decades. In 1926, Morton and Ernestine Luchs bought the property, established the Luxmanor Corporation, and developed the Luxmanor subdivision. Fortunately, the Riley house and surrounding acreage were left untouched.

In 1936, Luxmanor Corporation sold the Riley house to William and Levina Bolton, who lived in the house until 1950. During their first three years in the home, the Boltons made substantial renovations to make the house suitable for modern living. They added a section to accommodate a modern kitchen and bathroom, replaced both exterior and interior surface materials, removed and added porches, and changed the spacing of windows and the location of doors.

The remodeling of the house, done in the Colonial Revival style typical of the time, was designed by Lorenzo Winslow. A famous architect, Winslow was the White House architect for two decades; of his many contributions to the Washington, D.C., area, he is most noted for the design of the East Wing of the White House.

During the renovation of the Riley/Bolton House, most of the original rough-hewn logs in the log room were not replaced, but the floor was elevated, the loft and the stairway accessing it were removed, and a connection between the house's dining room and the log wing was added.

Because of the substantial alterations to the house since the Rileys had inhabited it, the house became designated the Riley/Bolton House. In 1950, Levina Bolton and her sister-in-law, Edna, who were joint tenants, sold the house to William and Harriett Coburn.

When the Coburns purchased the property, some outbuildings—including, perhaps, slave quarters—remained. It's unclear if the buildings had been maintained during the Boltons' tenure on the property, if the Colburns later removed them, or if they simply collapsed from neglect and the debris was cleared.

In 1963, Marcel and Hildegrande Mallet-Prevost purchased the Riley/Bolton House. They owned the house for more than forty years until they sold it to Montgomery County in 2006. In 2011, the house was listed in the National Register of Historic Places.

JOSIAH HENSON SPECIAL PARK

Montgomery County purchased the Riley/Bolton House and 1.43 acres of the surrounding land for $1 million in 2006 with the goal of creating a park dedicated to educating people about Josiah Henson, the history of Montgomery County, and the institution of slavery in Maryland.

After Harriet Beecher Stowe's novel *Uncle Tom's Cabin* was published in 1852, Josiah Henson became associated with the hero of the novel, due both to similarities between the novel's plot and Henson's life and to personality traits shared by Henson and the fictional Uncle Tom. Henson and Uncle Tom became so closely intertwined in the public's imagination that Henson's third and fourth autobiographies include references to Uncle Tom in their titles, and when Henson met Queen Victoria late in life, she referred to him as Uncle Tom.

Because of Henson's connection to the literary Uncle Tom, the park was originally named Uncle Tom's Cabin Special Park. The park's name,

Left: Josiah Henson Park sign. *Photo by Sonja Scharles.*

Below: Log wing of the Riley/Bolton House. *Photo by Edna M. Troiano.*

however, caused confusion. People assumed that "Uncle Tom" had lived in the log wing of the house. But Henson was enslaved on the property and would not have lived in the log wing—although on his return from Kentucky, he said that he spent a few miserable nights there, sleeping on the dirt floor of the kitchen.

The only people who might have lived in the log kitchen on the Riley plantation would have been cooks, who probably slept in the kitchen's loft, which was removed during remodeling. Henson would have lived in separate slave quarters that no longer exist. Furthermore, the slave quarters would have been shared by many of the enslaved workers. As Henson said, up to a dozen huddled together in a single room.

In 2008, the age of the log wing was determined using a method called dendrochronology—examining core samples of some of the cabin's logs to determine their age. The study concluded that the log structure was built around 1850. By that time, Henson had been living in Canada for twenty years. In 2010, the park was renamed with a more appropriate title, the Josiah Henson Special Park.

The Josiah Henson park is under the umbrella of the Maryland–National Capital Park and Planning Commission, an agency that serves both Montgomery and Prince George's Counties. In 2006, the park opened for visitors for the first time on June 24 and 25. Currently, the park is open only for special events and for group tours offered through Montgomery County's History in the Parks program.

On November 1, 1864, Maryland's new constitution emancipated the enslaved. November 1, designated Emancipation Day, commemorates that event. Emancipation Day is celebrated annually at the Josiah Henson Special Park by an open house in which Keenan Holmes, archaeology program assistant and museum docent, introduces visitors to the park. Every February during Black History Month, Holmes gives guided tours titled "A Walk in Father Henson's Footsteps." On both occasions, Holmes introduces visitors to Henson's life, slavery in Maryland, the Riley/Bolton House, and the ongoing archaeological excavations that help disclose the history of the Riley plantation.

Montgomery Parks offer field trips for students in grades four through eight. When children get off the bus, Holmes said that they inevitably ask the same three questions: Are there ghosts on the plantation? Where are the bodies buried? Did the enslaved live in the house? As they enter the house, Holmes briefly explains historic preservation as he introduces students to Henson and discusses slavery in Maryland. Younger students may know little about slavery, and even the older students—who usually have some knowledge of slavery, the Underground Railroad, and major figures such as Douglass and Tubman—know little about Henson.

Since most students are unfamiliar with archaeology, Holmes explains the ongoing excavations at the site and familiarizes them with basic terms and processes. For students, the most exciting part of the field trip is a simulated archaeological dig in which students unearth an artifact similar to those found at the site—nails, pottery shards, clay marbles—from a box of soil. Students also take part in a ceramic mending activity, piecing together

Left: Keenan Holmes. *Photo by Marilyn Sklar.*

Right: Cassandra Michaud. *Photo by Logan Devoe.*

broken plates. For students, the day is informative and enjoyable. For many of the teachers and chaperones who accompany the students, the field trip is transformative, expanding their knowledge of slavery and introducing them to Henson, the largely unknown hero who lived in their region of Maryland.

From May to December, volunteers under the guidance of Cassandra Michaud, the co-lead of the archaeology program, excavate the land twice a week, looking for artifacts and attempting to locate outbuildings. Michaud said that more than twenty thousand artifacts have been unearthed. The artifacts cover the period the land was occupied, roughly from 1800 to 2006. The focus of their study, however, is the period from 1800 to 1865, when the land would have been worked by the enslaved.

The area will eventually be graded to allow for landscaping. Before that occurs, county archaeologists are exploring the grounds, trying to reconstruct the areas. They have located a large area that seems to be a building of undetermined type. They know that the Riley planation is likely to have included a smokehouse, forge, barns, and sheds, as well as quarters, but archaeologists have not yet been able to confirm the location of these structures.

During an average year, the school groups and public events draw between 750 and 850 visitors to the park. The number of people who visit the site is increased, however, by those who walk or drive past, notice archaeologists and volunteers working at the dig, and stop by to watch the process and sometimes even to join in.

TIME TEAM AMERICA

Time Team America, a public television series, created archeology-based documentaries with the tension, flair, and excitement of reality television. From 2009 to 2014, a team explored nine sites, one of which was the Josiah Henson Special Park. In each documentary episode, a team of archaeologists, scientists, and historians explored intriguing American historic sites for three days, hoping to learn more about the land and the people who inhabited it and maybe even solve some archaeological mysteries.

In 2012, *Time Team America* filmed at the Henson park on August 13–15. Through research, the team hoped, in Montgomery Park's historian Dr. Cheryl La Roche's words, "to emancipate Josiah Henson one more time."

Using remote sensing technology that allows archaeologists to see underground and create 3-D models, the team, joined by Montgomery County archeologists, explored the park's grounds to isolate the areas to be explored. The goal was to find evidence of Henson's life by looking primarily for slave quarters and exploring the house's log wing. Although the park was a mere acre and a half, a small portion of the land that would once have been farmed by Riley, the team hoped that outbuildings might have clustered around the main house, as these structures did on many plantations.

On the first day, the team attempted to find evidence of buildings that might be slave quarters and looked for a trash pit, always a rich source of archaeological evidence. At the trash pit, they unearthed ceramics of varied types and ages, items typifying everyday use.

Since the team knew that Isaac Riley was a blacksmith, they could assume that one of the outbuildings would have been a forge. Furthermore, the forge would probably have been built near a barn since Riley would have made horseshoes and nails for his own horses, as well as to sell to the public.

Looking for the slave quarters, the team discovered a layer of compacted soil, which indicates a dirt floor—a clear sign of a structure. Further excavation on that site revealed bottle glass and ceramics—signs of an inhabited place but not conclusively of slave quarters.

On the second day, the team began the search for the blacksmith shop and started to explore the log wing, which they thought offered the best chance of finding evidence of Henson. The log kitchen once clearly had a door to the outside, as evidenced by vertical cuts in the logs. That door would have enabled fieldworkers to come for food without entering the log room. Other spots higher on the log walls indicate where joists probably supported a loft where the cook and her family slept.

Although this kitchen was built in 1850, about twenty years after Henson arrived in Canada, it could have been built over an older floor, so the team members pulled up a large central portion of the floor to see what was beneath. The floor they removed, probably from the 1970s, revealed boards from an earlier period, probably the renovation of the 1930s. Underneath that floor, dirt was visible.

On the third day, the team continued to look for the blacksmith shop and the slave quarters, sift through the trash heap and look for an older kitchen. Although the team members discovered wrought nails that may have been forged in the blacksmith shop, there was no definitive archaeological proof that they had discovered the site of the forge.

In the kitchen, the team found a thin concrete floor, probably dating from the early twentieth century, under the first layer of dirt. On the concrete floor, they discovered an old corroded flatiron near the fireplace, where it would have been heated before being used to iron clothes and linens. Beneath the layer of concrete was a layer of soft soil, and beneath that, a layer of compact soil, suggesting it served as a dirt floor, probably from the era when Matilda Riley had the wing built. Finally, they reached a lower layer of compact soil; this could be, the team agreed, the floor that Henson actually walked on and perhaps slept on when he returned briefly from Kentucky in 1829.

All *Time Team America* explorations were limited to three days—the time in their title referring both to going back in time and to the speed with which the teams worked. When they left, the outdoor excavations were filled in or covered. The archaeological search, however, is not finished; archeologists and volunteers from the Maryland–National Capital Park and Planning Commission continue to work each year on finding clues to the life of Henson and the role of slavery in Maryland.

THE FUTURE OF THE JOSIAH HENSON PARK

In 2009, the park acquired a second parcel of land, bringing the park acreage to 2.78 acres. In June 2017, the Montgomery Planning Board proposed the county provide $880,000 to purchase an additional 0.57 acres of land, currently owned by J. Emlen Myers. The total site, 3.35 acres, will more than double the original park space and provide for ongoing archaeological discoveries.

The Maryland–National Capital Park and Planning Commission plans to convert the ground floor of the Riley/Bolton House to a museum with interactive exhibits about plantation life, enslaved people, and Josiah Henson. The upstairs will contain a research library about slavery in Maryland as well as an office. Outside, the former garage will become a visitors' center and a pavilion for school groups.

Chapter 3

DAVIESS COUNTY, KENTUCKY

On the Road

The prolonged lawsuits and countersuits between Isaac Riley and Arnold Thomas Windsor, the man who had married George Riley's widow, Mary, lasted for years and weakened Isaac Riley's financial situation.

Isaac's wife, Mathilda, was so parsimonious that her younger brother, Francis, now Riley's ward, sometimes fled to Henson for food because he wasn't given enough to eat, an ironic reversal of slaveholders eating well while providing inadequate food to the enslaved. Matilda's attempts at economy, however, were offset by what Henson referred to as Riley's "continual dissipation," the habitual drinking and gambling that resulted in brawls like the one that led to Henson's maiming.

The combination of the ongoing lawsuits, the lack of fiscal responsibility, and what Henson referred to as general incompetency finally led Riley to the brink of bankruptcy. Riley feared that he would lose everything—his home and land, his enslaved, and all his other assets.

Henson's attitude toward Riley mingled pity, pride, and scorn. His Christian faith gave him compassion for Riley's troubles and his pride made him eager to embrace the role of counselor, but his description of Riley's character reveals his contempt:

> *Harsh and tyrannical as my master had been, I really pitied him in his present distress. At times he was dreadfully dejected, at others, crazy with*

drink and rage. Day after day would he ride over to Montgomery Court House about his business, and every day his affairs grew more desperate. He would come into my cabin to tell me how things were going, but spent the time chiefly in lamenting his misfortunes and cursing his brother-in-law. I tried to comfort him as best I could. He had confidence in my fidelity and judgment, and partly through pride, partly through that divine spirit of love I had learned to worship in Jesus, I entered with interest into all his perplexities. The poor, drinking, furious, shiftless, moaning creature was utterly incapable of managing his affairs.[37]

In January 1825, the situation came to a crisis: Riley was told that in two weeks he would have to sell all his enslaved workers to pay off his debts. Filled with self-pity, Riley turned to Henson for help, admitting that he had often abused him and offering the feeble excuse that he hadn't really intended to. Henson was torn between pity for Riley and terror at the prospect of his family being separated and sold. Riley demanded that Henson promise to help him before he would reveal what that help would entail. Riley rightly assumed that once Henson gave his word, he would follow through, no matter how daunting the task.

The way out of his dilemma, Riley had concluded, was for his enslaved to no longer be on the plantation when the sheriff came to seize them. The easiest way to accomplish that would be to send them to his brother Amos's plantation in Daviess County, Kentucky. Riley would supply Henson with a pass (a document signed by a slaveholder giving the enslaved permission to travel) and would follow them in a few months to Kentucky, where he could start fresh.

For Riley, it seemed a simple solution to his financial problems. For Henson, it entailed leading his wife, Charlotte; his two small sons, Tom and Isaac; and eighteen of Riley's enslaved workers on a journey of one thousand miles through unfamiliar territory and over mountains on foot in the dead of winter. When Henson hesitated, Riley reminded him of the other option: his family separated and sold, probably to the Deep South, where conditions for the enslaved were far more abysmal.

Since childhood, Henson had taken pride in the confidence that other people had in him, and given this enormous responsibility, he admitted, "My pride was aroused in view of the importance of my responsibility, and heart and soul I became identified with my master's project of running off with his negroes."[38] As overseer, he had earned the trust of the workers. They were used to obeying him, and they were grateful for the many ways he had made their lives more bearable. Also, like Henson, they realized that walking to Kentucky, arduous though it was, was vastly better than being separated and sold to the Deep South.

With a one-horse wagon stocked with supplies for both the horse and the people, they walked away from Montgomery County. The first day, they left around 11:00 p.m. and didn't pause until noon the next day. The men were on foot, and the women and children sometimes in the wagon, sometimes walking.

Since 1805, when he had been sold and transported to Montgomery County as a child, Henson had never traveled farther than a few miles from the Riley plantation where he sold produce in the markets of Montgomery County, Georgetown, and Washington, D.C. Now, with twenty-one people depending on him, he led the way through Culpepper and Fauquier County, Virginia, to Harper's Ferry, West Virginia, and then to Cumberland in Western Maryland. The route they followed, a terrain challenging in all seasons, was daunting in winter. At Cumberland, they were able to take the recently opened National Pike across the mountains, where they traveled alongside pioneer families headed west.

Along the way, Henson encountered other groups of the enslaved traveling with overseers. While overseers typically chained their enslaved together to prevent them from escaping, Henson was able to leave his unbound, knowing that they would be loyal and remain with him. When questioned, he showed the pass Riley had provided. His explanation that he was leading Riley's slaves to Kentucky repeatedly brought about praise. Henson said that "often was the encomium of 'smart nigger' bestowed on me, to my immense gratification."[39] Being entrusted to such a complicated mission by Riley and having praise heaped upon him along the way reinforced his determination to fulfill his mission. Ironically, that commitment led to what he later admitted was the worst decision he made in his life.

When they reached Wheeling, West Virginia, at the Ohio River, Henson sold the horse and wagon as Riley had instructed and bought a boat. The plan was to follow the Ohio River to Amos Riley's plantation in Owensboro, Kentucky. When the boat neared the Ohio shore, people along the river's edge encouraged them to come ashore and be free. At Cincinnati, crowds of free black people gathered to urge them to join them, telling them that they "were fools to think of going on and surrendering [themselves] to a new owner" when they could land in Ohio, a free state.[40]

That moment marked a crisis of conscience in Henson's life. As the urge to rebel arose among the men, even Henson began to waiver. Henson had always assumed that he would someday be able to buy his freedom, but he had never planned to run away. His religion, through the sermons he had heard, convinced him that fidelity to his master was God's will and that running away was a form of theft.

The other factor in his decision to continue down the river was his pride and his love of praise. He had promised Riley that he would deliver the enslaved to Riley's brother Amos, and he was determined to keep his word. He admitted, "I had undertaken a great thing; my vanity had been flattered all along the road by hearing myself praised; I thought it would be a feather in my cap to carry it through thoroughly, and had often painted the scene in my imagination of the final surrender of my charge to Master Amos, and the immense admiration and respect with which he would regard me."[41]

The enormity of his decision to continue on to Kentucky haunted him throughout the years. He admitted, "Often since that day has my soul been pierced with bitter anguish at the thought of having been thus instrumental in consigning to the infernal bondage of slavery, so many of my fellow-beings."[42] He prayed for forgiveness, all the more fervently after he became free and therefore more aware of what he had denied the others.

Henson remained unable to resolve the conflict between what he considered his Christian duty to keep his word and obey his master versus considering the well-being of those in his charge. He finally admitted that he personally had lost many opportunities by not remaining in Ohio when he had the chance. But he still prided himself on his decision, saying, "The perception of my own strength of character, the feeling of integrity, the sentiment of high honour, I thus gained by obedience to what I believed right, are advantages which I prize."[43] He finally reconciled the contradiction between the wrongdoing of keeping people enslaved and the importance of keeping his word by laying the blame on the long-term effects of slavery that engrained unquestioning obedience in the enslaved.

DAVIESS COUNTY

In mid-April 1825, Henson and his companions reached Daviess County, referred to by Henson in his autobiographies as Davis County. Daviess County was created in 1815 when it was carved out of Ohio County, Kentucky. The new county was named for Joseph Hamilton Daviess, an attorney who had gained fame prosecuting Vice President Aaron Burr for treason in 1806.

Active in the Kentucky militia, Daviess participated in several expeditions against Native Americans. He became a colonel under the command of William Henry Harrison, who catapulted into national fame at the Battle of Tippecanoe in Indiana in November 1811. The Battle of Tippecanoe pitted Governor Harrison of the Indian Territory against a confederacy of Native Americans led by the Shawnee leader Tecumseh. Because the British had sided with the Native Americans by providing arms and financial support, the relationship between the Americans and the British deteriorated. Six months after the Battle of Tippecanoe, the United States declared war on Britain, marking the beginning of the War of 1812. The battle was so important that when William Henry Harrison ran for president in 1840, his campaign song was "Tippecanoe and Tyler Too." However, the battle that launched Harrison's political career ended Daviess's: he died in the Battle of Tippecanoe.

LIFE ON AMOS RILEY'S PLANTATION

Amos Riley's plantation was much larger than his brother Isaac's. Consisting of about ten thousand acres divided into five farms, the plantation stretched from the Ohio River to Yelvington, about ten miles northeast of Owensboro, with Riley's house located five miles south of the Ohio River near the center of his lands. The land was also more fertile than at his brother's plantation.

Isaac had sent all twenty-two of his enslaved workers: Henson, his wife, his two children, and eighteen others. Amos Riley, Henson estimated, held between eighty and one hundred enslaved laborers who were housed in log cabins along the river, separated from the plantation by a row of Osage orange trees. Amos Riley's farm produced more food than his brother's plantation, and the enslaved people were better fed. As he had done in Maryland, Henson served as farm superintendent, saving Amos Riley a substantial sum of money.

Since his conversion at Newport Mill, Henson had been a pious, devoted Christian. Even his determination to lead the enslaved to Amos Riley's plantation instead of freeing them in Ohio had been, in his view, a Christian act of keeping one's word. In Kentucky, as overseer, he had more freedom, and he used that time to hear preachers and attend camp meetings. By

Harvesting corn. *New York Public Library.*

listening to others preach and by observing the reactions of the listeners, he learned how to engage an audience and sway them emotionally. In 1828, Henson was admitted as a preacher in the Methodist Episcopal Church. He could not have anticipated at that juncture in his life that he would become known as Father Henson and would preach in churches in the United States, Canada, and England.

Before Henson started the trek to Kentucky, Isaac Riley told him that he and his family would follow in a few months. Three years later, in the spring of 1828, Henson learned that Isaac Riley, unable to persuade his wife, Matilda, to move to Kentucky, would remain in Maryland. Isaac Riley had lost much of his farmland through mismanagement and lawsuits and no longer needed many slaves. He sent an agent to sell the eighteen enslaved workers whom Henson had brought to Kentucky and told Amos to send Henson and his family back to Maryland with the money from the sale.

Isaac Riley's motive for not selling Henson and his family, Henson said, was to get him back to work on the Maryland farm: since Henson had left, Riley's land had been increasingly less productive, and he was desperate to keep what little he had. Amos Riley, on the other hand, was reluctant to give Henson a pass to travel because Henson managed his farm well and spared him the salary of an overseer.

With the sale of his enslaved companions imminent, Henson felt the crushing burden of his decision to continue to Kentucky instead of freeing them in Ohio. He recalled the auction that separated him from his siblings and his mother when he was a child. Although he could not save the others, he resolved to become free, saying, "One absorbing purpose occupied my soul—to gain freedom, self-assertion, and deliverance from the cruel caprices and fortunes of dissolute tyrants." To obtain that goal, he "stood ready to pray, toil, dissemble, plot like a fox, and fight like a tiger."[44]

Henson was well aware of the abolitionist movement. John McKenny, the man whose preaching had led to his conversion, was widely known to be an abolitionist. In Henson's early trips to sell produce in the markets in Montgomery County, Georgetown, and Washington, D.C., he would have frequently heard people talking about the growing movement to free the enslaved. But while Henson had yearned to be free, he had also intended to earn his freedom rather than run away. Many of the enslaved hoped to earn the money to buy themselves, and many others hoped to gain freedom eventually through the gratitude of their owners. Both methods often failed.

An unexpected opportunity arose in the summer of 1828 between the time Henson learned the enslaved were to be auctioned off in Kentucky and the time he left to return to Maryland. A Methodist preacher developed a friendship with Henson, visiting him often. Finally, the man spoke to Henson in confidence and revealed his purpose; he told Henson that because of his abilities, he should be free, not enslaved. Furthermore, he had in mind a scheme that would enable Henson to buy his freedom.

Henson never named this preacher, referring to him simply as a "kind friend." This preacher gave him his first hope of attaining freedom and also set him on the path to becoming known as Father Henson, famed for his preaching. Some abolitionists, like Harriet Tubman and Frederick Douglass, became famous. Others, like John McKenny, were widely known regionally. However, many preferred to stay in the shadows. A person might face threats or even violence from neighbors or a community if known—or even suspected—to be an abolitionist. Moreover, once someone was suspected of being an abolitionist or of colluding on the Underground Railroad, that person's every movement could be suspect, hindering their usefulness to the cause. If Amos Riley had known the preacher friend who often visited Henson intended to enable Henson to buy his freedom, Riley would have undoubtedly forbidden him to visit Henson and might also have refused to provide Henson with a pass to return to Maryland.

His friend advised Henson to ask Amos Riley for permission to return to Maryland to see Isaac Riley again. The crops in Kentucky had already been brought in, so Henson wouldn't be needed in the fields. Henson assured Riley he would be back long before he was needed for spring planting. Riley naïvely accepted that Henson would be willing to travel a distance of almost two thousand miles round-trip to visit the man who had abused him so badly.

Amos Riley wrote a pass allowing Henson to travel between Kentucky and Maryland as the servant of Amos Riley. The Methodist preacher who had developed the plan gave Henson a letter of recommendation to carry to a colleague in Cincinnati, Ohio, and also agreed to accompany him there. Upon arrival in Cincinnati, the preacher in turn introduced Henson to others who invited him to preach in several of the Cincinnati churches. Exhilarated by the prospect of being able to buy his freedom and feeling for the first time that he had control over his own destiny, Henson pleaded his circumstances to the congregations. Saying that it was "an issue of life and death, of heaven and hell," he implored people to make contributions.[45] When he left Cincinnati, he had accumulated $160.

Still accompanied by the preacher, Henson's next stop was Chillicothe, where he attended the Methodist Episcopal Church's Ohio Conference. On his friend's advice, Henson bought a good suit and a horse. As he traveled from Kentucky to Maryland, he continued to preach and request funds for his self-emancipation. By the time he arrived at the Riley plantation, he had earned $275.

Henson arrived at the Riley plantation, well dressed and on horseback—better dressed, he said, than Isaac Riley. Henson explained that the horse and the clothes were needed for the preaching he did along the way, but he could see Riley's irritation. A commonly repeated belief among slaveholders was that "uppity" slaves, those who were suspected of thinking they were in any way superior or had any rights, should be immediately disabused of the notion, so Riley immediately began to make clear his power over Henson.

First Riley checked and seized the pass, which gave Henson the right to return to Kentucky, and asked his wife to put it away for safekeeping. Henson was alarmed, realizing that if he had no pass, he would have to remain on Isaac Riley's plantation instead of returning to Kentucky. Then he was told he was to sleep on the dirt floor in the kitchen, already crowded with the enslaved. They were all strangers to him. From them, he learned that his mother had died, severing all personal ties he had with the place.

Instead of giving in to despair, Henson plotted a way forward. He decided to appeal to Frank, the younger brother of Riley's wife, Matilda, who as a boy had often fled to Henson for food and comfort when Riley abused or underfed him. The morning after his arrival, Henson asked Matilda for his pass so he could go to Washington to visit Frank. Riley had already gone to the tavern, so he was able to speak to her privately. She hesitated, but Henson convinced her that without the pass he could be imperiled should anyone stop him and demand to see his papers.

Frank remained fond of Henson but hated Riley, not only for mistreating him as a boy but also for taking property he believed he should have inherited. Henson confided his plan to buy his freedom to Frank, who agreed to intercede on Henson's behalf and negotiate a deal for Henson's freedom.

Frank arrived at the plantation a few days later and urged Riley to allow Henson to buy his freedom. He made the case that Henson had served the family faithfully for years and had been key to Riley's financial success. He argued that Henson had paid for himself already in the amount of produce he managed to grow. Then he put forth a more practical and convincing argument. Since Henson had his pass, which would allow him to leave unimpeded, and since he had money and a horse, he was already close to independence. If Riley didn't allow Henson to purchase his freedom, Henson might escape, leaving Riley with neither slave nor cash.

Riley and Frank came to a verbal agreement: Henson would pay a total of $450 to Riley and receive his manumission papers. Before returning to Kentucky, Henson would pay $350 in cash. He would send the remaining $100 he owed Riley later. Henson had already earned $275 through preaching on his way from Kentucky to Maryland. He needed an additional $75 to reach the amount Riley required, so he sold his horse. Since Henson had already earned money by preaching, he probably assumed he would be able to earn the remaining $100 the same way.

Henson received his manumission papers on March 9, 1829, and prepared to leave for Kentucky the next morning. As he was getting ready to leave, Riley approached him and asked if he intended to show his manumission papers if anyone stopped and questioned him. When Henson said that he would, Riley warned him that it would be dangerous to do so because anyone could take the manumission papers from him, even a slave trader. His traveling pass would be adequate to guarantee a safe passage. To ensure that the manumission papers remained safe, Riley offered to put them in an envelope addressed to his brother and put three wax seals on it, adding that no one would break a seal since it was illegal and could result in a prison sentence. Henson said he felt grateful for Riley's concern and put the sealed manumission papers in his carpetbag. What Henson did not know was that the original manumission papers had listed the cost of freedom as one dollar, a sum to which Riley had added three zeroes.

Because he had sold his horse, Henson walked to Wheeling, West Virginia, a distance of about 255 miles. Henson states matter-of-factly that he was arrested several times along the way—an incident that any black person traveling alone would face—but each time he insisted on appearing before a magistrate and was allowed to continue because of his pass. At Wheeling, he caught a boat to take him along the Ohio River.

When Henson reached the plantation, he went straight to the cabin to see his wife and children. His happiness at their reunion was brief. Charlotte had somehow learned that the price Isaac Riley had demanded for her husband's freedom was $1,000, and she immediately asked him how he intended to raise such a large sum. That was when he realized he had been deceived. Riley had changed the terms of the agreement, changing the price of his freedom from the $450 they had verbally agreed upon to $1,000. Henson had given Riley all his money, $350. In order to be free, he would need to pay an additional $650—an impossible sum for him to raise.

Before Riley convinced Henson to let him seal the manumission papers in an envelope addressed to his brother Amos, Henson had possession of the papers. However, Henson was illiterate. If he had been able to read, he might have detected the ruse and been able to appeal again to Frank. By sealing the papers, Riley had ensured that Henson wouldn't be able to show them to anyone along the route.

From the slaveholders' vantage point, keeping the enslaved illiterate was crucial. Although literacy was already rare among the enslaved, in 1740 South Carolina passed the first laws that prohibited slave education. In the mid-eighteenth century, laws in southern states proliferated against teaching the enslaved to read or write. Slaves who could write could forge their own passes so they could travel unimpeded, the easiest way to escape. They could read abolitionist tracts and learn of opportunities to escape, people who would assist them, and places where they might be safe. They could circulate notes fomenting and organizing rebellions. They could learn which states were free and how much better conditions were in the North. In the case of Henson, his illiteracy allowed him to be swindled out of all his money and his opportunity to buy his freedom.

There were exceptions to enforcing illiteracy. In some places, the enslaved were encouraged to read the Bible or receive religious education on the assumption that they would be more docile if they knew the Bible condoned slavery, condemned violence, and offered a final reward in heaven for those who accepted their lot. Others of the enslaved were taught to keep records so they would be more useful workers. Both of these reasons for allowing limited education for the enslaved were, of course, primarily to the advantage of the slaveholder.

Now that Henson was back at Amos Riley's Kentucky plantation, he was helpless. Because he was illiterate, he couldn't write to Frank. He couldn't enlist anyone to help him write a letter because the only people he knew who could read and write were slaveholders. He described himself as alternately "beside [himself] with rage, and paralysed [*sic*] with despair."[46]

He knew that Amos Riley must not get possession of his manumission papers, so when he greeted him the next morning, he said he had lost them. Riley, aware of his brother's scheme to swindle Henson, seemed relatively unperturbed by the loss. Seeming amused, he taunted Henson, saying, "Want to be free, eh! I think your master treats you pretty hard, though. Six hundred and fifty dollars don't come so easy in old Kentuck. How does he ever expect you to raise all that? It's too much, boy, it's too much." He then dismissed the theft, saying, "Well, boy, bad luck happens to everybody, sometimes."[47]

Cheated out of his money and his freedom, Henson found himself working on the plantation again. His strength of character after this crushing blow echoes his reaction after his maiming: "I went about my work with as quiet a mind as I could, resolved to trust in God, and never despair."[48]

The enslaved had reason to live in fear of the slaveholder, but many slaveholders also feared the enslaved. Despite their lack of power, the enslaved sometimes found retribution through poison and arson, both nearly always untraceable. In many agricultural areas, the enslaved far outnumbered the slaveholders, creating an atmosphere of anxiety among slaveholders. The most famous uprising was that of Nat Turner, who on August 21, 1831, led a group of six enslaved men, enlisted about seventy-five others, and murdered more than fifty white people before the rebellion was squelched. As a result of Turner's uprising, laws for the enslaved became harsher and limited freedoms even more restricted.

Henson reported that in 1830, a year before the Turner rebellion and only months prior to his escape, the enslaved in a large area encompassing the Amos Riley plantation had planned an insurrection. The plan was for some of the enslaved at all the plantations involved to set fire to houses and barns at 11:00 p.m. on a set date. As the slaveholders and their families fled their burning houses, they would all be killed. Henson knew that the enslaved had "provocation enough to rise and take the places of their masters," but he dissuaded the participants on the grounds that although slavery was horrific and the enslaved deserved freedom, their plan was neither feasible nor Christian. Furthermore, he argued that the uprising would worsen the plight of the enslaved, saying, "Suppose we killed one thousand of the white population, we would surely lose our own lives, and make the chains of those in bondage heavier and more securely riveted. No, let us suffer in God's name, and wait His time for Ethiopia to stretch forth her hands and be free."[49] The uprising did not take place, and we can assume that the slaveholders never heard a rumor of it, or there would have been swift and harsh retaliation.

New Orleans, Louisiana

For months after Henson's return from Maryland in 1829, Amos Riley occasionally taunted Henson about the $650 he was supposed to raise. Since Henson, enslaved by Amos's brother Isaac, was providing free labor, the arrangement was advantageous to both brothers: Isaac had the $350 he had swindled from Henson, and Amos had the free labor that would have been his brother's.

One day, Amos Riley surprised Henson, telling him that his son, Amos Jr., would leave the following day to take a flatboat loaded with livestock and produce down the river to New Orleans. Henson would accompany him and help with the sale of the goods. The conditions for enslaved workers in the Deep South were even more abysmal than in the Upper South, and the possibility of being taken to New Orleans, the country's largest slave market, would have terrified any enslaved person.

Eli Whitney's 1793 invention of the cotton gin, which removed the seeds from cotton after it had been picked, made cotton a far more profitable crop. Increased production of cotton required an increased labor pool, driving the growth of slavery in the South.

Ten years later, in 1803, the country acquired approximately 827,000 square miles from France in the Louisiana Purchase. This vast new tract of land created an enormous demand for labor. Five years later, in 1808, the government outlawed transatlantic and international slave trade. Since the enslaved could no longer be imported from Africa or the Caribbean,

River flatboats. *New York Public Library*.

enslaved laborers had to be sought within the country. The rising demand for enslaved labor resulted in increased prices, and it was common for slaveholders in the Upper South, in states such as Kentucky, to sell their enslaved "down the river."

The need for increased labor in the Deep South and the new territory created a forced migration of the enslaved from other parts of the country. The demand was so great that many were sold before they even left the boat. In New Orleans, as in most cities with large auction sites, the enslaved were kept in slave warehouses or pens—open-air cells or shanties about the size of a house lot that enclosed up to one hundred men, women and children. In *Uncle Tom's Cabin*, Stowe described a typical slave warehouse: "A slave-warehouse in New Orleans is a house externally not much unlike many others, kept with neatness; and where every day you may see arranged, under a sort of shed along the outside, rows of men and women, who stand there as a sign of the property sold within."[50] Since many of the enslaved were emaciated, they were well fed after their arrival so they would look healthy and fetch higher prices. They remained in the pens or warehouses until they were sold or auctioned off.

Slave warehouse. *Library of Congress.*

New Orleans's position on the Mississippi River made it accessible from many parts of the country. At one point, there were more than fifty slave markets in the city. One slave auction took place in the rotunda of what is now a popular tourist site, the Omni Royal Orleans Hotel in the French Quarter.

Henson had good reason to assume, since he was headed to New Orleans, that he would be sold. The only preparation he made was to have his wife sew his sealed manumission papers into some cloth and then sew the cloth into the waist of his jacket. Although the manumission papers were currently worthless since he was unable to pay off his debt, he thought they might help him if he could escape.

Henson did not know what prompted the decision to sell him, but he knew that Isaac and Amos Riley had been writing to each other frequently. The sale may have been prompted by Frank's warning in his discussion with Isaac when they agreed to the terms of manumission: Isaac should either let Henson buy his freedom or risk his escape, in

Auction in New Orleans Hotel Rotunda. *Wikimedia Commons.*

which case he would gain nothing. Isaac hadn't allowed him to buy his freedom; he had the $350 he had defrauded Henson out of, but he could make far more money from Henson's sale. Since Isaac Riley had ongoing financial problems, and since he received no labor from Henson, he may have initiated the sale out of financial need. The decision to sell Henson may also have been prompted by the competing claims between the two brothers—Henson was enslaved by Isaac, but Amos had the profit of his labor. They may have decided to end their quarrel by selling Henson and sharing the profit.

Henson was desolate, thinking that he might never see his wife and children again, but it didn't seem to occur to him—or he didn't mention the possibility—that if he was gone from the plantation, his wife and children might also be sold, probably separately, as he was when he was a child.

The boat's crew consisted of Amos Jr., three unnamed white men, and Henson. The typical procedure on a journey was to sell items as the boat progressed, stopping wherever they would reap a good profit. The cargo, Henson said, included cattle, pigs, poultry, corn, whiskey, and miscellaneous articles. Henson, the crew knew, was the most valuable part of the cargo.

Since Henson was the only enslaved person on the boat, he was required to take three shifts at the helm for every one shift by any of the others. As in his other endeavors, both his work ethic and his pride in accomplishment are evident. He said, "I learned the art of steering and managing the boat far better than the rest. I watched the manoeuvres necessary to shoot by a 'sawyer' [an uprooted tree still attached to the bank], to land on a bank, avoid a snag, or a steamboat, in the rapid current of the Mississippi, till I could do it as well as the captain."[51] His pride in his ability to maneuver the boat was at odds with the mission; he strove to excel at an activity that was bringing him closer to personal catastrophe.

Because the captain was the only one who knew the river, only he could pilot the boat at night. During the voyage, the captain developed inflamed swollen eyes and eventually became temporarily blind. Although they could no longer travel at night, they continued during the daylight hours, and Henson said he was "master of the boat" all the way to New Orleans.

When the boat docked at Vicksburg, Mississippi, Henson received permission to visit a nearby plantation where some of Isaac Riley's slaves had been sold. He now faced the consequences of the decision he had made when he insisted on continuing to Amos Riley's plantation instead of freeing his colleagues in Ohio. He described the lives of his former colleagues: "Four years in an unhealthy climate and under a hard master had done the ordinary work of twenty. Their cheeks were literally caved in with starvation and disease. They described their daily life, which was to toil half-naked in malarial marshes, under a burning, maddening sun, exposed to poison of mosquitoes and black gnats, and they said they looked forward to death as their only deliverance." He called it "the saddest visit I ever made" and realized it was also a portent of what his life might become after he was sold in New Orleans.[52]

Seeing how emaciated and miserable his former colleagues were made Henson realize that he, being older than they were, would be unlikely to survive long under the same conditions. At this point, the faith that had sustained him throughout his ordeals briefly left him; unable to pray or hope, he felt that God had abandoned him. In his anger, Henson contemplated all he had done for the Riley brothers over the years. He had taken enormous pride in all the praise they gave him. He had been loyal to them, and now he realized how empty their praise was. Their willingness to sell him, he said, "turned my blood to gall, and changed me from a lively, and, I will say, a pleasant-tempered fellow, into a savage, morose, dangerous slave."[53]

From Henson's point of view, he deserved not to be sold for all the good work he had done. For Isaac Riley, he had increased the farm's productivity, sold his produce for a profit, and even transported his enslaved so he would not lose them. He had, in short, probably saved the Riley plantation. He had enriched both Isaac and Amos Riley by serving as an unpaid skilled overseer. Now he could even pilot a boat on the Mississippi. All the skills he had worked hard to attain meant to the Rileys only that he had increased his market value and selling him was a wise financial move.

As they neared New Orleans, Henson decided that since the Riley family intended to shorten his life, he should get revenge by shortening the lives of those who would destroy him. He planned to kill the four men aboard, scuttle the boat, and escape. Although he realized that the plan was likely to fail, he said he was "blinded by passion, and stung to madness."

A few days before they were due to reach New Orleans, an opportunity to carry out his plan arose. Amos and the three crewmen were asleep below deck. Henson silently descended and grabbed an axe. In the dim light, he saw Amos, who was nearest him, and lifted the axe. At that instant, he suddenly realized the enormity of what he intended: he was a Christian and he was about to commit murder. He had been thinking of the act as justifiable self-defense. Now he realized he had been about to kill a young man who was only obeying his father and who had never personally harmed him. He also believed that committing the crime would negate all he had done to develop his character and live by Christian principles.

He put down the axe and retreated, thanking God, as he said he has done every day since, that he did not commit murder. No one on the crew ever suspected how close they came to death. Back on deck, he resolved to resign himself to the will of God, whatever it might be, and "to die with a Christian's hope, and a quiet conscience." Once again, he had put his principles over his self-interest.

When they arrived at New Orleans, the remaining cargo was sold and the crew dismissed, and as soon as Henson could be sold, the boat was to be broken up and the lumber sold. Amos would return to Kentucky by steamboat. Amos's charge was not only to sell Henson but also to get the best possible price. Henson said that when planters came to see him, "I was sent on some hasty errand that they might see how I could run; my points were canvassed as those of a horse would have been; and, doubtless, some account of my various faculties entered into the discussion of the bargain, that my value as a domestic animal might be enhanced."[54]

Henson repeatedly begged Amos not to sell him, reminding him of all he had done for his father, as well as the things he had done for his Uncle Isaac. He talked about the misery of the enslaved from Isaac Riley's plantation who were now in Vicksburg. Amos sometimes was sympathetic, but other times he swore at Henson and hit him; mostly, Amos avoided Henson.

The night before Henson was to be sold, Amos became ill. Henson called it "one of those sudden, marked interpositions of Providence, by which in a moment, the whole current of a human being's life is changed." Amos's illness progressed rapidly, and by the following morning, he was helpless. The two men's situations were now reversed: Henson said, "I was no longer property, no longer a brute-beast to be bought and sold, but his only friend in the midst of strangers."[55] Amos begged Henson not to abandon him. He asked him to sell the boat, gather the trunk containing the profits from the sales, get him onto a steamboat, and accompany him home. Henson said Amos was near death and so weak he could barely speak or move. A less ethical man than Henson might well have left Amos to die, kept the proceeds, and attempted to make his way north to freedom.

Once on board the steamboat, Henson watched over Amos, fed and cared for him. As he had forgiven Isaac Riley years ago for his many beatings and abuses, he now forgave young Amos, saying, "All remembrance of personal wrong was obliterated at the sight of his peril."[56]

The return voyage along the Mississippi and the Ohio took twelve days. When they reached Amos Riley's plantation on July 10, Amos Jr. was still too weak to walk, so Henson arranged for him to be carried to the house on a stretcher borne by a relay of the enslaved. The Riley family was initially effusive in their praise of Henson, both for saving their son and for bringing back the profits earned through sales during the voyage.

Henson returned to his work on the plantation. Amos's recovery was slow; he was too weak to leave his room until mid-August. Although Amos Jr. remained grateful and admitted that he would have died without Henson's care, the others in the family no longer expressed any gratitude or appreciation.

Henson realized that his loyalty, his service, and his accomplishments had increased his market value, but not the Rileys' loyalty. They would soon try again to sell him. He had always intended to purchase his own freedom and had never tried to escape when the opportunity occurred. But now, to avoid being "sold down the river," he had to escape. Even in these dire circumstances, Henson felt obligated to justify his decision, explaining, "If Isaac had only been honest enough to adhere to his bargain, I would have adhered to mine, and paid all I promised. But his attempt to kidnap me again, after having pocketed three-fourths of my market value, in my opinion, absolved me from all obligation to pay him any more, or to continue in a position which exposed me to his machinations."[57]

HENSON'S HERITAGE IN KENTUCKY

Unlike the sites where Henson once lived in Maryland and in Canada—La Grange, Josiah Henson Special Park, and Uncle Tom's Cabin Historic Site—there is no historical site marking Henson's life on Amos Riley's Kentucky plantation.

The 1883 work *History of Daviess County* mentions neither Amos Riley nor Josiah Henson. The omission could be because Henson had lived in Kentucky for only three years and had escaped to Canada nearly five decades before the book was written. He was, however, famous throughout Canada and England by that time and well known among heroes of the Underground Railroad. He was also widely reputed to be the inspiration for the character of Uncle Tom in Harriet Beecher Stowe's *Uncle Tom's Cabin*, a controversial book many county residents would have read and almost all would have heard about.

The year after the Daviess County history was published, Judge Amos Riley Jr., the man who had taken Henson on the flatboat trip to New Orleans decades before, gave an interview to the *St. Louis Post-Dispatch* that was reprinted in the *Owensboro Messenger & Examiner* on September 10, 1884. Riley began by expressing his surprise at receiving a copy of the *London Times* and discovering that Henson, a celebrity in England, had spoken at length about him and his family. Riley described Henson's story as a "spirited" account of what he "purports to be the story of his early life."

Amos Riley Jr.'s account differs from Henson's in several ways. Riley said that his Uncle Isaac sent Henson with his other enslaved to Kentucky not because of his debts, but because his brother Amos's glowing descriptions of his plantation persuaded Isaac to relocate. Riley added that when he was young, he often worked in the fields with Henson but could not keep up with him because Henson's arms and shoulders were so powerful. Speaking of the New Orleans trip, Riley said he and Henson were both excited because Amos Riley promised them the profits of all sales over $400; they were both so eager to go that they set out almost immediately. The trip was uneventful, and they both returned to work on the plantation. When Isaac Riley asked that his enslaved workers be sold and Henson and family returned to Maryland, Amos Riley paid the costs of their journey, but Henson never returned. The family assumed that when Henson reached Cincinnati, he decided to head for Canada instead of Maryland.

Riley dismissed most of Henson's story as a combination of inaccuracies and fiction. Of Henson's relation to Uncle Tom, Riley theorized that Henson was clever enough to recognize a story he could twist to his own purposes. Riley's version is simply that a strong, clever servant ran away; it's a common story, unremarkable in every aspect, so it's unsurprising that Henson aroused little interest in Daviess County in the nineteenth century.[58]

In the last half of the twentieth century, Henson's connection to Daviess County was discovered by chance, and Henson became the focus of widespread local interest. In 1967, Edith Bennett and her father were traveling in Canada when their car broke down. The car was towed to a garage in Dresden, Ontario, where two mechanics, having noticed Daviess County printed on their Kentucky license plates, recommended they visit the nearby Uncle Tom's Cabin Historic Site. Bennett and her father toured the museum, the Henson house, and the Henson family cemetery, where they learned about the connection between Henson and Daviess County.

At around the same time, Dr. M. David Orrahood, a history buff and a physician at the Owensboro–Daviess County Hospital, spoke with Susan Hawes, the great-granddaughter of Amos Riley. During the conversation, Hawes mentioned that Riley had owned Josiah Henson, the model for Uncle Tom.

Upon her return to Kentucky, Bennett told Hugh Potter, her supervisor and manager at the local radio station, about her discovery. Potter was skeptical until he spoke with Orrahood. The three of them collaborated and did additional research, and on October 22, 1967, they revealed their findings about Henson's connection to Daviess County in the local newspaper, the *Owensboro Messenger-Inquirer*.[59]

Jack Thomson, the curator of the Dresden museum, visited Owensboro that same year, and years later, in 1989, Bennett traveled to the Uncle Tom's Cabin Historic Site in Dresden for its celebration of what would have been Henson's 200th birthday.

The discovery of the connection between Henson and Daviess County attracted the attention of Joe Sparks, an electrician and avid local historian, who in a 1980 interview with *The Gleaner*, a Henderson, Kentucky newspaper, said he'd been fascinated by the story since he learned about Henson in 1967. Over the years, Sparks amassed material about Henson

Josiah Henson Trail historical marker. *Photo by Rich and Cindy Stierwalt.*

and the history of slavery. He became one of the strongest advocates for restoring the Amos Riley plantation as a park dedicated to Henson.[60]

In 1970, the Kentucky Historical Society erected a roadside marker (no. 1241), titled "Uncle Tom Lived Here," on U.S. 60, just east of Maceo near the site of Amos Riley's former plantation. The marker reads, "Site of Riley family home place, owners of Josiah Henson, one of the characters on which Harriet Beecher Stowe based her 1852 novel *Uncle Tom's Cabin*. Henson served as overseer of Amos Riley's farms, 1825–29. On learning [his] owner planned to sell him 'down the river,' he escaped to Canada, living there [the] rest of [his] life. Invited to visit Mrs. Stowe in Andover, Mass., 1848."

Ten years later, on September 16, 1980, county judge William J. Froehlich of Daviess County signed a proclamation declaring that September 18, 1980, would be known as Josiah Henson Day in the county. The date marked the 150th anniversary of Henson's escape to Canada. Judge Froehlich lauded Henson's character and his achievements, concluding that Henson is recognized as one of the most nationally significant historical figures to have lived in the Commonwealth of Kentucky.

Of Henson's character, Froehlich said that Henson "treated his fellow man with respect, and courtesy, and was always willing to go a little further in attending the needs of those less fortunate than himself" and that he "carried on a considerable religious work, bore unmerited suffering, with christian patience, possessed integrity, and christian character, manifested under extraordinary and difficult circumstances." Of Henson's accomplishments, Froehlich cited his work as an abolitionist, his immortalization in Stowe's *Uncle Tom's Cabin*, his establishment of a vocational school for escaped slaves, and his meeting with famous people, including Queen Victoria, the prime minister of England, the Archbishop of Canterbury, and President Rutherford B. Hayes.[61]

One year later, in 1981, the Owensboro–Daviess County Chamber of Commerce received a federal grant of $15,000 for a feasibility study to develop a site on the land that was once Amos Riley's plantation. Ideas for developing the site in honor of Henson included reconstructing a slave cabin, expanding the site to include a museum, and adding a summer theater where Stowe's *Uncle Tom's Cabin* could be performed.[62] Two years later, the chamber determined that the cost of acquiring land, developing the site and maintaining it would be prohibitive.

On June 14, 1989, the day that would have marked Henson's 200th birthday, the section of U.S. Route 60 stretching from Owensboro to the Hancock County line at Blackford Creek was officially named the Josiah Henson Trail.

On September 12, 1992, Owensboro's new River Park Center held a benefit gala. One of attractions of the evening was a preview of a new musical drama, *Josiah!*, based on Henson's life. The following year, *Josiah!* played at the River Park Center for six nights, drawing an audience of four thousand.[63]

In June 2013, the Owensboro Museum of Science and History purchased a collection of seventy-five historic documents at a Cincinnati auction for $6,500. The papers were the personal documents of Amos Riley and his son, Camden Riley. The collection contains sales and business receipts, including documents detailing sales of the enslaved. There is also a slave pass allowing Henson to have "safe and unhindered passage" to and from Yellow Banks (the early name of Owensboro) and Riley's plantation at Yelvington for purposes of plantation business.[64]

In 2015, on the 200th anniversary of the founding of Daviess County, a new history was published: *Daviess County, Kentucky: Celebrating Our Heritage, 1815–2015*. In the book's chronology of two hundred events, one paragraph lists major events in Henson's life and highlights his connection to Harriet Beecher Stowe's novel. The only other mention of Henson is incidental: in a discussion of the significance of the Ohio River, the author mentions the voyage to New Orleans when Henson accompanied Amos Riley Jr., citing it as a typical example of the flatboat trade.

Throughout the last half of the twentieth century, Henson had gone from being largely unknown to being a subject of local curiosity and pride, before then fading to being an incidental note in Daviess County history.

Chapter 4

ESCAPE

THE FUGITIVE SLAVE ACTS

Attempting to escape bondage required enormous courage. History records the stories of many who succeeded, but the stories of those who failed usually disappeared from the pages of history. When slaveholders discovered a missing slave, they immediately put up posters and ran newspaper ads describing the fugitive and offering rewards. Slave catchers, who made their living by pursuing and capturing fugitives, were in high demand. And many people would report unfamiliar black people they noticed in their area on the chance that they might be escapees.

When escapees were caught, the price for failure was great. Once returned to their slaveholders, they faced brutal punishment. They might be flogged, branded or maimed—sometimes through hobbling, for example, by having their Achilles tendons severed. They might be fitted with a device that hindered movement, such as an iron collar welded around their neck with long spokes protruding that would prohibit them from running through deep woods or even leaving the plantation without being recognized as a former fugitive. They might be jailed. They might be sold into the Deep South—the situation Henson was desperate to avoid. They might also, as an object lesson to other enslaved, be killed, sometimes publicly in a horrific way.

Aiding a fugitive also came at a price. In 1793, the United States Congress enacted the first Fugitive Slave Act, which required all states—both free

A wanted poster. *Wikimedia Commons.*

and slaveholding—to capture and return escapees who had fled to another state. The act also imposed penalties on anyone aiding a fugitive. Despite widespread resistance, Congress passed a second Fugitive Slave Act in 1850, when Henson was safely in Canada. The second Fugitive Slave Act was far more draconian: it required citizens to aid officials in the capture of escapees and imposed penalties for any official who didn't arrest a person accused of being a runaway or any citizen who aided a runaway by doing as little as providing food or shelter.

Although legal penalties for aiding a fugitive were usually restricted to a fine and a jail sentence, there were social penalties as well. Those known or even suspected to have aided escapees might be ostracized or forced to leave town. They might face acts of retribution, such as the boycotting or burning down of their businesses. Their homes and their every move might be under surveillance by slave hunters and vigilantes. In some cases, especially in the Deep South, the penalty for helping fugitives was death.

Penalties varied widely but were far harsher in the Deep South than in the Upper South or the North. Captain Robert Lee, who was arrested helping fugitives escape from Norfolk in his boat, was sentenced to twenty-five years in the Richmond Penitentiary. In 1844, Jonathan Walker, who was captured trying to help a group of escapees sail to freedom in the Bahamas, was jailed for only one year. However, Walker was also branded on the palm of his hand with "SS," which stood for "Slave Stealer." The branding took place in the courthouse, where a fire had been lit for that purpose.

THE UNDERGROUND RAILROAD

The Underground Railroad system helped an estimated 100,000 people escape from bondage. The name Underground Railroad began to be widely used in the 1830s, when Henson had just arrived in Canada. The origin of the expression paralleled the building of actual railroads. As the term gained popularity, other railway terms were attached to it. Safe houses became "stations" or "depots," and "stationmasters" hid the escapees, often in their homes. The escapees using the Underground Railroad were "passengers," "freight," or "cargo." "Agents" connected those wanting to escape to the Railroad, "conductors" were the Railroad's guides, and "stockholders" provided financial support.

Long before anyone had heard of an Underground Railroad, people had been working together to aid fugitives from enslavement. In 1786, George Washington complained about the loss of two slaves, one his own. The problem in retrieving runaways, Washington complained, was that Quakers were known to conspire to help fugitives escape. Even though Henson was unlikely to have heard the expression Underground Railroad, he was familiar with abolitionists and how their networks helped fugitives. During his time in Montgomery County, he had heard the abolitionist John McKenny preach, and he would have heard about abolitionist activities when he sold produce in the markets of Georgetown and Washington, D.C. When his "dear friend" in Kentucky encouraged him to earn money to buy his freedom, as well as when he traveled through Ohio preaching, he would have encountered many abolitionists. When Henson was helped along the way to his destination in Canada, he became part of the network that was soon to be known widely as the Underground Railroad. He, of course, would have had no idea that years later he would become an important part of the Underground Railroad when he repeatedly left Canada at his own peril and returned to the United States to help others flee slavery.

Anyone willing to feed, shelter, or help a runaway in any way was part of that system; it began with the establishment of American slavery and lasted until emancipation. As the system grew, some regions had well-organized antislavery groups and a system of routes and routines. For example, Levi Coffin, a Quaker in Indiana who was dubbed the "President of the Underground Railroad," is believed to have helped as many as three thousand escapees pass through his Indiana home.

In other areas, the Underground Railroad was more loosely—and sometimes even haphazardly—organized. And some instances of helping runaways were spontaneous acts of mercy that might never be repeated. Because of the severe penalties for both those escaping and those aiding them, the danger was real. Secrecy was crucial, and many of the early efforts to help the enslaved are still shrouded in secrecy.

The National Park Service summed up the complexities and contradictions inherent in the Underground Railroad: "The Underground Railroad story is like nothing else in American history: a secret enterprise that today is famous, an association many claim but few can document, an illegal activity now regarded as noble, a network that was neither underground nor a railroad, yet a system that operated not with force or high finance but through the committed and often spontaneous acts of courage and kindness of individuals unknown to each other."[65]

Although escaping through the Underground Railroad suggests a uniform experience, the enslaved who reached freedom told remarkably varied stories. Two of the best known come from the slave narratives of Frederick Douglass and Harriet Jacobs.

In his 1845 autobiography, *The Narrative of the Life of Frederick Douglass*, Douglass refused to explain his escape, partially to avoid creating difficulties for those who helped him but also because explaining his route to freedom might "run the hazard of closing the slightest avenue by which a brother slave might clear himself of the chains and fetters of slavery."[66] By 1881, when he published *The Life and Times of Frederick Douglass*, slavery had been abolished, so he was free to divulge how he had fled. In 1838, unable to travel without either a pass or manumission papers, Douglass borrowed a Seaman's Protection document, which proved that he was a free American citizen. He had worked on boats and knew that he could, if necessary, talk convincingly about boats and seafaring. Wearing the clothes of a typical seaman—a red shirt with a loosely tied black scarf and a tarpaulin hat— he boarded the train in Baltimore. When the conductor asked to see his manumission papers, he showed his seaman's certificate and was allowed to continue. In Wilmington, Delaware, he disembarked and took a steamboat to Philadelphia. That same night, he boarded another train to New York. Although Douglass had spent years contemplating his journey to freedom, he said that the actual trip took only twenty-four hours.[67]

While Douglass escaped in one day, Harriet Jacobs's path to freedom took years. Jacobs, writing under the pseudonym "Linda Brent" in *Incidents in the Life of a Slave Girl*, told of ongoing sexual harassment by her slaveholder, Dr. Norcom. Because Harriet continued to refuse to become his mistress, she was sent to work on his son's plantation, about which she said, "I would rather drudge out my life on a cotton plantation, til the grave opened to give me a rest, than to live with an unprincipled master and a jealous mistress."[68] She had two children by an unmarried white lawyer, but by law, the children of the enslaved were also enslaved. When she learned that Dr. Norcom planned to put her children to work on the same plantation, she decided to escape, hoping that the children's father would protect them. After she escaped, she was hidden by friends—both black and white—but the search for her was too persistent and the situation too perilous for her and for those who concealed her. She then moved into a crawlspace above a shed that had been added to her grandmother's house. The space was nine feet long, seven feet wide and three feet at the apex. There was neither light nor fresh air, but since it had a concealed trapdoor, it was a relatively safe hiding place. Jacobs stayed hidden in that tiny space for seven years before she escaped. In 1842, she was able to get to Philadelphia by boat and then, shortly after, to New York by train. Jacobs was eventually reunited with her children. Both Jacobs and Douglass, having obtained their freedom, became abolitionists, working to free other enslaved people.

Because secrecy was crucial to the success of the Underground Railroad and the safety of both the fugitives and those who helped them, written records are scarce. However, one man, William Still, wrote down narratives that would otherwise have gone unrecorded, providing for posterity stories of the courage, ingenuity, and endurance of fugitives. Born a slave in 1821, Still became free when his father bought his freedom. In 1844, he moved to Philadelphia, Pennsylvania, in a free state, and soon became active in the abolitionist movement. Because Philadelphia was the first major city north of the Mason-Dixon line, which separated slave states from free states, many fugitives headed there. When Still became chairman of the Vigilance Committee of the Pennsylvania Anti-Slavery Society in Philadelphia, he provided temporary shelter for refugees passing through on the Underground Railroad. He helped an estimated eight hundred refuges on their paths to freedom and was often called the "Father of the Underground Railroad."

As the refugees came to Still's home, he recorded their stories. Still knew how difficult it was for families to reunite, especially if their names had been changed or if family members had been enslaved in different locations or by different slaveholders. In hopes that the families could eventually reconnect, Still wrote down their stories, including where and by whom they had been enslaved. After emancipation, he published these narratives in *The Underground Railroad*.

One of Still's narratives tells of Anna Maria Weems, a fifteen-year-old girl who, like Henson, had been enslaved by Adam Robb in Montgomery County, Maryland. In 1855, in order to escape, Weems was smuggled into Washington, D.C., and hidden for weeks. Still arranged for his family doctor to travel to Washington and bring Weems back to Philadelphia. She disguised herself as a man, assumed the name Joe Wright, and traveled in the guise of the doctor's coachman. She had to sound and act like a male in order to deceive everyone they encountered, but she succeeded and reached Philadelphia undiscovered.

One of the most ingenious escapes recorded was that of Henry Brown. Brown knew that he could get help from abolitionists in Philadelphia but didn't know how to get there. In 1849, with the help of two sympathizers, he arranged to be shipped from Richmond, Indiana, to the Anti-Slavery Society in Philadelphia, Pennsylvania, in a box that was nailed shut and bound with strips of hickory wood. Because of his daring escape, he became known as Henry "Box" Brown.

Many of the escapes Still documented required extraordinary endurance. In 1859, Henry Cotton fled to a secluded swamp deep in a forest, where he lived for a year, even temporarily hiding in the hollow of a tree. He was aided only by his brother, who managed to bring him a little food occasionally. He stayed undetected for the entire year, surviving a harsh winter, before he was able to escape.

Henson's escape was made eight years before Douglass's and almost thirty years before Cotton's. On his odyssey from Kentucky to Canada, he exhibited the same strength, cunning, and endurance of many of the fugitives whose struggles to freedom Still documented.

HENSON'S PATH TO FREEDOM

Because the 1793 Fugitive Slave Act authorized local governments to capture and return runaways, even reaching a free state was no guarantee of safety. The abolitionists Henson had met in Ohio had convinced him that Canada was the only place where he could be confident of remaining free. Because escaping often required enormous physical strength and stamina, most escapees were relatively young men who traveled alone. Henson said that if he had been single, he would have set out and followed the North Star, like so many before him. The enslaved hoping to escape were taught that if they would follow the North Star, it would lead them to the free states and to Canada. For Henson, the North Star was the "God-given guide" that, like the star at Bethlehem, would lead to salvation. He said, "I knew that it had led thousands of my poor, hunted brethren to freedom and blessedness. I felt energy enough in my own breast to contend with privation and danger; and had I been a free, untrammeled man, knowing no tie of father or husband, and concerned for my own safety only, I would have felt all difficulties light in view of the hope that was set before me."[69]

Henson, however, was determined not to desert his family. If he was to be free, then his wife, Charlotte, and their children must also be free. Henson developed a plan, but when he confided his intentions to his wife, she was terrified, saying, "We shall die in the wilderness, we shall be hunted down with bloodhounds; we shall be brought back and whipped to death."[70] Her fears were not exaggerated; those were the experiences of many escapees.

Henson's attempts at persuasion were futile. Finally, he said he would leave, taking the three oldest children with him and leaving only the youngest with her. He had arrived back in Kentucky from New Orleans in mid-July, and it was now mid-September. If he stayed on the Riley plantation, he would soon be sold, so either way the family would be torn apart. After a long night of entreaties and arguments, he left for work in the morning, only to hear Charlotte call him back to say she and the children would flee with him. That was on a Thursday, and Henson decided to leave on the following Saturday.

The most common time for the enslaved to run away was Saturday after work. Because Sunday was not a workday, they might not be missed until Monday morning, giving them a little over a day's head start before their absence was noticed. There was another advantage to Henson's choice to escape on Saturday: the Riley plantation was a conglomeration of farms that stretched from the Riley's house to the Ohio River. Henson was overseer on all the farms, and on Monday and Tuesday, he was scheduled to be on farms that weren't close to the Riley house. As a result, the family might have at least three days before Riley would know they were missing and begin the hunt. Henson's cabin was near the river's landing, another advantage in quickly escaping across the Ohio River.

The major difficulty would be transporting four children, especially the two youngest, two-year-old Peter and three-year-old Josiah. Henson had devised a plan—he would carry them on his back to Canada, a distance of about five hundred miles. He had asked Charlotte to sew a large bag made of tow cloth with sturdy straps for his shoulders. To prepare for the trip, he practiced walking at night carrying Peter and Josiah in the sack. The two older children, Tom and Isaac, would walk with Charlotte.

One complication remained: the couple's oldest son, Tom, lived in Amos Riley's house. Henson had to gain Riley's permission for Tom to leave the house so the entire family would be able to flee. On Saturday, Henson went to Riley's house and reported on his work, as usual. As he left, he seemed to

Henson escaping with his family. *Uncle Tom's Cabin Historic Site.*

suddenly recall something; he turned and told Riley that his wife had asked if Tom could come home for a few days so she could "mend his clothes and fix him up a little." The request seemed so innocuous that Riley didn't hesitate to give permission for Tom to leave.

That night, they set out on the first leg of their journey, across the Ohio River from Kentucky to Indiana. The night was dark and moonless, which increased their chance of crossing the river undetected. The man rowing the skiff, another of Riley's enslaved whom Henson had persuaded to help them, was nervous and asked, "It will be the end of me if this is ever found out; but you won't be brought back alive, Sie, will you?"[71] Henson assured him that he did not intend to be brought back, but that even if he was captured, he would never, under any circumstances, reveal the name of the man who had helped the family set off on their journey to freedom. That rower later also made his way to freedom in Canada, and Henson said that they often discussed that night on the river.

Due to a growing abolitionist movement, when Indiana became a state in 1816, the state constitution outlawed slavery. Four years later, the Indiana Supreme Court freed all the remaining enslaved. Even though Indiana was a free state, Henson knew that Southern Indiana was still perilous for fugitives. He described the area as "bitterly hostile to the fugitive." Many residents were proslavery, and slave catchers sometimes patrolled the shoreline. Henson knew that there was no time to linger on the shore; before dawn, they would have to walk as many miles as possible and be safely hidden in the woods or risk being arrested and returned. With no friends to assist the family, Henson said that God was their only hope.

From Southern Indiana, they headed northeast to Cincinnati, Ohio. The family continued to walk for two weeks, Henson carrying the two younger children on his back and his wife walking with the older two. They walked on a road at night, ducking into a hiding place if they heard a horse or a vehicle approach. During the day, they stayed hidden deeply in the woods.

They were only a two-day walk from Cincinnati when they ran out of food. Exhausted and hungry, the children cried all night, and Charlotte reproached Josiah for leading them into such a wretched situation. Henson said that had he been alone, he would have weathered the hunger and exhaustion rather than leave his hiding place, but he had an obligation to care for his wife and children. He, too, was exhausted, and his back and shoulders were rubbed raw from carrying the children. Moreover, whenever he slept, he would awake suddenly, his heart pounding, thinking that dogs and slave catchers had discovered them.

To feed his family, Henson had to leave his hiding place and go out on the open road. To allay suspicions that he was a runaway, he headed south. At the first two houses where he stopped to ask if he could buy food, he was rudely turned away by men who said they would never offer any help to a black person. At the third house, the man also refused to sell him food, but his wife intervened, arguing that she would feed a hungry dog and that their children might sometime need the help of a stranger. The woman refused his money and supplied him with venison and bread.

Because the venison was so salty, the children became thirsty. Henson went in search of water, breaking bushes as he went so he wouldn't get lost. He finally found a stream and drank. When he tried to carry water back in his hat, it leaked. His solution was to rinse out his shoes, which fortunately had no holes, and use them to carry water back to his family. Later in life, he reminisced about that night, saying, "I have since then sat at splendidly-furnished tables in Canada, the United States, and England; but never did I see any human beings relish anything more than my poor famishing little ones did that refreshing draught out of their father's shoes."[72] Having eaten and drunk, they headed off on that night's walk.

After walking for two more nights, the family reached Cincinnati. Ohio had outlawed the buying or selling of the enslaved in the state constitution when it was granted statehood in 1802. In 1804 and 1807, the state had enacted "black laws" in an attempt to stem immigration and restrict opportunities for black people, but these laws were rarely enforced at the time. Although Ohio was technically a free state, it wasn't until 1841 that any enslaved people brought into the state automatically became free. As black fugitives flooded into Cincinnati in the first decades of the nineteenth century, racial tensions escalated. In July 1829, the year before the Henson family arrived, Cincinnati began to enforce the "black laws." That same month, rioting erupted with whites attacking blacks, burning their homes and, in many cases, capturing both free black people and escapees and selling them into slavery. Because of the riots, more than one thousand black people fled Cincinnati.

Fugitives from Kentucky, Virginia, or the Deep South headed for Ohio because of the river; for hundreds of miles along the northern border of Kentucky and the western border of Virginia, the Ohio River marked the boundary between slavery and freedom. Because of the 1793 Fugitive Slave Act, Ohio was still dangerous territory for escapees, and there was strong anti-abolition sentiment and high racial tensions among the citizens. But it was also a state with a well-organized Underground Railroad with many stations along the route to Canada.

In Cincinnati, for the first time, Henson felt relatively secure. He was in a free state, and he had contacts who would help him along his journey. Before walking into town, he hid his wife and children in the woods. After he found his friends, who welcomed him into their safe house, he returned to the woods just before nightfall and retrieved his wife and children. This was the first time since they stepped into the skiff on the river the night they left Kentucky that they felt safe. Henson noted, "Two weeks of exposure to incessant fatigue, anxiety, rain, and chill, made it indescribably sweet to enjoy once more the comfort of rest and shelter."[73]

Henson said that the abolitionists who sheltered and protected fugitives on the Underground Railroad were widely despised. He, however, lauded those "who, through pity for the suffering, voluntarily exposed themselves to hatred, fines, and imprisonment." For Henson, they were following the dictates of Christ. He cited Matthew 25, in which Christ praises whoever feeds the hungry, gives the thirsty drink, provides clothes to the naked, and visits the sick or imprisoned, explaining, "Inasmuch as ye have done it unto the least of these My brethren, ye have done it unto Me."[74]

They stayed in the safe house until they recovered their strength. Then the family was transported for thirty miles away from Cincinnati in a wagon. The next leg of their journey, again on foot, was to Scioto County in south-central Ohio, slightly under one hundred miles. As before, they had to travel at night and hide during the day.

From Scioto County, Henson had been told to take a road made by General Hull during the War of 1812. For the first time, they were able to travel during the day. However, the road was seldom used after the war, and it was overgrown and nearly impassable. Henson had made a miscalculation; he had taken almost no food or drink, assuming that he would be able to get some along the way. But they were traveling through underbrush on an overgrown, uninhabited wilderness road. At night, in addition to being exhausted and hungry, Charlotte and the children were terrified by the howling of wolves. They were relatively safe from wolves, who rarely attacked groups, but most escapees traveled alone, and attacks by wild animals were a real danger.

The next morning, Henson divided a portion of the only remaining food, a small piece of dried beef—enough to increase their thirst, he said, but not enough to ease their hunger. That day's trek was arduous. Henson said, "The road was rough, the underbrush tore our clothes and exhausted our strength; trees that had been blown down, blocked the way; we were faint with hunger, and no prospect of relief opened up before us. We spoke little, but steadily struggled along; I with my babes on my back, my wife aiding the two other children to climb over the fallen trunks and force themselves through the briars."[75] Weak from exhaustion, Charlotte passed out when trying to climb over a log. After a few minutes, she revived. He fed her a few remaining bites of beef, and the family struggled on. Although Henson encouraged his family, he realized that they might all starve to death in the wilderness, as other fugitives had.

In the midafternoon, they saw people approaching in the distance. When they got a little closer, Henson could see they were Indians. He realized that if they were hostile, trying to escape would be futile, so he continued to walk toward them. When the Indians saw the Henson family, they looked alarmed, turned, and with "a peculiar howl" began to run in the opposite direction, continuing for a mile or two. Charlotte was frightened, too, thinking that the Indians had gone back to collect others and that the group would return and murder them. She urged Henson to go back, but he refused, saying that there were enough Indians to murder them if that was their goal, but it would be foolish for the two groups to run from each other. As they continued, the forest became quiet, and soon they saw Indians peering at them from behind trees, ducking back when they thought they were spotted.

Soon the Hensons came upon several wigwams. A "fine-looking stately Indian," seemingly the chief, awaited their approach, greeted them in English, and called the others in from the woods. The Indians presumably had never seen black people and were curious, reaching out to touch the children, who jumped back and shrieked with fear, causing the Indians to also shrink back. Once the novelty was over and they were accustomed to each other, Henson was able to explain where they were going and what they needed. The Indians generously fed the family and gave them a wigwam to sleep in.

The next morning, they set out again. The Indians told them that they were about twenty-five miles from Lake Erie, and some of the young men accompanied them to the point where they had to turn off the road. The Indians' provisions of food, shelter, and help in reaching the next step on the Hensons' journey was one of those spontaneous acts of mercy that made it possible for the Underground Railroad to aid so many of the enslaved.

As they neared Sandusky, located on Lake Erie, the land became flatter. Henson encountered a stream that flooded the road. To ensure that it was passible, Henson forded the stream alone, carrying a stick to check the water's depth. He first carried the two youngest children across, then the two oldest, one at a time, and finally his wife. By this time, he said, the skin was worn off his back from the weeks of travel with the children in his rough fiber knapsack.

Once again, they spent the night hidden in the woods. The next morning, as they approached Sandusky from the southwest, they were no longer in woods but in view of houses on a wide-open plain. About one mile from Lake Erie, Henson once again hid his family, this time in brush instead of in the deep forest, before going on alone.

Henson noticed a line of men walking back and forth between a house and a boat. When he approached, the captain called out to him, offering him a shilling per hour if he'd help load the boat. At first, the captain thought Henson too crippled to work, but Henson immediately grabbed a bag of corn and emptied it into the hold, proving his ability to do the job. He got in line next to a black man and asked the crucial question: how far away was Canada? Henson was fortunate; the boat was headed to Buffalo, New York. When the man next to him explained that Buffalo was just across the river from Canada, Henson confided that his wife and children were also traveling with him.

The man went to speak to Captain Burnham, who returned and spoke with Henson. He invited Josiah and his family to go on the boat, which would be sailing as soon it was fully loaded. When the captain pressed him, Henson admitted that he and his family were running away. Burnham initially told Henson to retrieve his family from hiding but then realized the danger. Slave catchers were common in the town, and anyone seeing Henson leading an exhausted wife and four children out of the brush might suspect they were fugitives. The captain told Henson to continue loading corn. Once the boat sailed, it would stop at an island close by and send another smaller boat back for Henson and his family.

Night was falling as Henson watched the boat set sail. As Burnham had promised, the boat pulled up to an island, and a small boat was lowered over the side. In ten minutes, two sailors and the black man Henson had met while loading the boat stepped ashore. The four men set out to find Charlotte and the children, but they were not where Henson had left them. Henson was terrified that his family had been discovered and kidnapped. Charlotte, when she heard several male voices, thought her husband had been captured, so she tried to hide from what she thought were slave catchers. Once she was reassured, the family and the men walked back to the boat—the final mile the Hensons would need to walk on their long journey to freedom.

When they climbed onto the deck of the boat, the crew cheered loudly, and the Scottish Captain Burnham told Henson, "Coom up on deck, and clop your wings, and craw like a rooster" for he would soon cross the water and become a free man. As the ship plowed through the water, Henson was overcome by emotion, saying, "Man and nature, and, more than all, I felt the God of man and nature, who breathes love into the heart and maketh the winds His ministers, were with us. My happiness that night rose at times to positive pain. Unnerved by so sudden a change from destitution and danger to such kindness and blessed security, I wept like a child."[76]

When they reached Buffalo the next evening, it was too late to cross the river, but Burnham pointed out a group of trees on the other side of the Niagara River, saying that as soon as Henson and his family reached those trees, they would be free. Burnham said he was poor and only sailed the boat for wages, but he would ensure that Henson reached Canada. Early on the following day, the captain gave Henson one dollar and asked a ferryman named Green to take Henson and his family across the river. The captain's only request was that Henson "be a good fellow," to which Henson responded, "I'll use my freedom well; I'll give my soul to God,"[77] a pledge he kept for the rest of his life.

On the morning of October 28, 1830, Henson, Charlotte and their four sons reached Canada and freedom. Henson described himself as so overcome with joy that he threw himself on the ground, rolling in the sand and kissing handfuls of it. When onlookers commented that they thought he was insane, he replied that he wasn't crazy—he was free. He hugged and kissed Charlotte and the children; their new life had begun.

They had fled Amos Riley's plantation in mid-September and arrived in Canada at the end of October, a six-week ordeal. They had eluded slave catchers, stayed free of debilitating diseases, avoided wild animals, and had faced starvation, exhaustion, and exposure to the weather. For a husband, wife, and four small children to have survived that ordeal was an amazing feat. During their trek through Ohio, they had been fed, sheltered, and shown the route to freedom by Quakers in Cincinnati, Native Americans in the Ohio wilderness, and a Scottish captain and his crew in Buffalo. The Underground Railroad, that unofficial network of highly organized antislavery groups and chance encounters with people of courage and integrity, had delivered another family to freedom.

Chapter 5

CANADA

THE FIRST YEARS

The Hensons had reached their goal: freedom. Yet the family still had struggles. They had no place to live, no money and no food, nor any way of attaining these. Henson paid the remainder of the dollar he had received from the captain to a family with whom they could spend their first night in Canada. The next morning, Henson left Charlotte and the children and set out in search of work. Within the day, he heard of a Mr. Hibbard who owned a large farm about six miles away in the Waterloo area. Farmers with large tracts of land often leased portions to tenant farmers, who would repay the landowner either in cash or in a portion of their produce. Although Hibbard's neighbors did not speak particularly well of his character, Henson, having been enslaved under Isaac and Amos Riley, was confident that he could satisfy Hibbard with "honest and faithful work."

He met with Hibbard, who agreed to employ him and supplied him with housing—a broken-down two-story shanty inhabited by pigs. Henson said he immediately drove out the pigs and began clearing and scrubbing the floor. By midnight, the floor was "in tolerable condition," and he slept in his newly acquired home. In under forty-eight hours, Henson had gone from being enslaved in the United States to being a free man in Canada with a job and a house.

The next morning, he brought Charlotte and the children to their new home on Hibbard's land. In addition to being old and rickety, the house was completely unfurnished. But the entire family was thrilled because their new house was so much better than the slave quarters where they had previously lived. Mr. Hibbard supplied Henson with straw, and Henson dragged logs into the corners and piled the straw three feet deep, making their first furniture, beds on which they, exhausted from their travels, "reposed luxuriously."

Henson's relief at their escape and subsequent good luck was tempered by the illness of Charlotte and all four children, no doubt a result of their long, arduous trek. Fortunately, all five eventually recovered, although Henson said that "it was not without extreme peril that they escaped with their lives."

Hibbard soon realized, like Isaac and Amos Riley had before him, that Henson was able to produce larger crops than others did on his property, and he grew to appreciate his most valuable employee. Hibbard's wife and Charlotte became friends. Henson said that food and fuel, the basics of life, were plentiful, and as a result of the friendship between the Hibbards and the Hensons, they also acquired what Henson described as "some of the comforts of life," perhaps for the first time.

Over the course of the next three years, Henson worked for Hibbard, sometimes for wages and sometime for shares of the produce he raised. He was able to buy some livestock—pigs, a cow, and a horse. When he stepped onto Canadian soil three years prior, he had absolutely nothing. Now he was free, and although he would still have been considered poor by some, he had more than he had ever had before.

Rev. Josiah Henson
Resident of Dresden, Canada,
The Original Uncle Tom
Of Mrs. Stowe will give an

Sla fe!

Pr e Forest,

This entertainment is given FREE to all, and all are invited to come and learn from the lips of this remarkable man (now 92 years old) what American Slavery has been to him.

UNCLE TOM'S CABIN
Dresden, Ontario, Canada

Father Henson. *Uncle Tom's Cabin Historic Site.*

A friend from Maryland who had recently moved to the area told others that Henson had been well known and admired for his skill as a preacher. Henson said he had not intended to preach, but simply to enjoy going to Sunday meetings. Now he felt called to preach again. Long ago, when he had sold Isaac Riley's produce in the markets in Georgetown and Washington, D.C., Henson said he had listened carefully to the educated men he encountered there and had learned and copied how they spoke. That early attempt at self-improvement was invaluable. Henson had little religious training, and because he was illiterate, he could not read the Bible or other religious tracts. Still, he said that he was "frequently called upon, not by blacks alone, but by all classes in [his] vicinity—the comparatively well educated, as well as the lamentably ignorant—to speak to them on their duty, responsibility, and immortality, on their obligations to themselves, their Saviour, and their Maker." His ability to preach so effectively stemmed from "not so much knowledge as wisdom; and observation upon what passes without, and reflection upon what passes within a man's heart, and will give him a larger growth in grace than is imagined by the devoted adherents of creeds."[78] Henson was now on his way to being known as Father Henson.

Hibbard and the local schoolmaster paid for a few school terms for Henson's eldest son Tom, who learned to read fluently. On Sunday mornings, Henson would ask Tom to select a random passage from the Bible and read it to him. Henson would memorize a few verses, or even a chapter, that he could use in his preaching. One day, Tom opened the Bible to Psalm 103: "Bless the Lord, O my soul: and all that is within me, bless his holy name." Both father and son were moved by the verse's beauty, and Tom began to ask questions: Who was David? Where did he live? When Henson was unable to answer his questions about the Bible, Tom finally realized that his father could not read.

When Tom proposed that his father learn to read, Henson said he could not because he had to work from daybreak to nightfall to feed his family and also because he could not afford a teacher. Tom offered to teach him, but Henson was ambivalent; he realized that being able to read would make him a better preacher, but it was hard for him to accept being taught by his twelve-year-old son. After spending the day in meditation and prayer, he realized that he ought to seize the opportunity. Father and son worked together at night by the light of a pine knob or hickory bark—the only light Henson could afford. Henson made slow progress, and he learned to read and write a little; he never, however, became adept at either and had to depend on others to write his letters, documents, and autobiographies.

Learning to read was a pivotal experience for Henson. He realized the "terrible abyss of ignorance" in his previous life and resented all the more the cruelty of keeping people illiterate and uninformed. He resolved to "do something for the rescue and the elevation of those who were suffering the same evils [he] had endured, and who did not know how degraded and ignorant they really were."[79] This resolution would lead to the greatest achievements of his life: the Dawn settlement and the British-American Institute.

After having worked for Hibbard for three years, Henson moved on. He described his new employer, Mr. Riseley, as "a man of more elevation of mind than Mr. Hibbard, and of superior abilities." Henson was still focused on helping the several hundred others who had escaped from slavery and were now living near him in Canada. He believed that their joy in their newfound freedom was so overwhelming that they were content to be tenant famers, as he had been for Hibbard. But Henson envisioned a greater possibility—that they could own their land and work for themselves rather than for other landowners. He also saw himself as the person who could bring the plan to fruition.

Riseley approved of Henson's plan and allowed him and a small group of about a dozen to gather at his house. The group agreed to pool their earnings and purchase land on which, Henson said, "every tree which we felled, and every bushel of corn we raised, would be for ourselves: in other words, where we could secure all the profits of our own labour."[80]

The Pre-Dawn Era

Henson's vision of a settlement created for the formerly enslaved was not the first such endeavor in Canada. In June 1812, President James Madison declared war on Britain. Shortly after, American troops invaded Upper Canada, the area that would become Ontario in 1867. The invasion was unsuccessful, and the United States troops were pushed back across the border. When American soldiers, sometimes accompanied by their enslaved personnel, returned from Upper Canada to the United States, the news spread quickly and widely that the enslaved could be free in Canada and that they would be safer than in the northern United States, where they could be captured by slave catchers. That awareness triggered waves of immigration into Canada.

During the first decades of the nineteenth century, fugitives flooded into Canada, many through Detroit, Michigan. Those who escaped across the Detroit River arrived in Windsor, Canada, which was only about seventy miles from what would become the Dawn settlement. The Upper Canada area was ideal for refugee settlements.

The Oro settlement, now Oro-Medonte, was established by the Upper Canada government in 1819. Oro was distinct from the other settlements that were developed primarily for black people because it was the only one designed by the Canadian government. The government offered land grants along Wilberforce Street in Oro Township to black veterans of the war, but free black people and the previously enslaved also settled there. The population of Oro came in two waves. The first was after the war, from Oro's inception in 1819 to 1826. The second wave, from 1828 to 1831, resulted largely from growing hostility and increasingly repressive fugitive laws in Ohio. It was at that perilous time that Henson and his family walked across Ohio from the Indiana border to Sandusky. Oro always remained small, with a population of black people never exceeding about one hundred. Due to the relatively poor soil, many of the original Oro farmers left and the settlement declined.

The racial turmoil in Cincinnati, Ohio, led to the founding of another early black settlement in Canada, Wilberforce, named for British abolitionist William Wilberforce. Free black people in Cincinnati formed a group to explore opportunities for emigration, and in 1828, two men, Israel Lewis and Thomas Crissup, met with the lieutenant governor of Upper Canada and agreed to purchase land from the Canada Company. After the Cincinnati riots of 1829, the first settlers—only five or six families—arrived. In 1831, the settlement began to grow rapidly, and by the following year, Wilberforce had schools, sawmills, a gristmill, and general stores. By 1835, Wilberforce's population reached 166, but it never topped 200. However, the settlement's growth was offset by the departure of some of the original leaders, who didn't adjust to a rural life after living in Cincinnati. Driven by the potato famine in the 1840s, the Irish immigrating into Canada moved to Wilberforce, the black population dwindled, and Wilberforce gradually disappeared as a black settlement.

Henson's concept was to create a settlement much like Wilberforce— one that would be built both by and for black people. Moreover, he wanted the settlement, like Wilberforce, to have a school to educate children and a means for citizens to earn a living. The first step in developing the settlement was to select land suitable for colonization and agriculture. On behalf of the group of refugees who had been meeting at Riseley's home and were interested in creating the new settlement, Henson set out on foot in the fall of 1834 to explore the land bordering Lakes Huron, Erie, and Ontario. Just to the east of Lake St. Clair, which is positioned between Lake Erie and Lake Huron, Henson found an area, Dawn, along the Sydenham River where the land was fertile and the climate relatively mild, making it ideal for farming and for colonization.

In *Stepping Back in Time*, Marie and Jeffrey Carter explored the development of Dresden, the town that would emerge from the area that encompassed the Dawn settlement. When Henson explored the area in 1834, it was sparsely populated: tribes of First Nations had lived in the area for centuries, and as early as the first decade of the century, some pioneer families had arrived in the vicinity. The area began to grow in the 1820s. In 1825, Jared Lindsey, a white man of European descent, built a home in the area that would later become part of Dresden. That same year, Weldon Harris and Levi Willoughby, two black men who were presumably refugees from the United States, arrived, and each bought fifty acres of land. All three men are listed on documents as living in Dawn. Although the settlement Henson would later establish in Dawn would be a beacon for black refugees, a small black community may well have already been established prior to the development of the Dawn settlement.[81]

When Henson returned to report on his finds, the group recommended that he return the following summer so that he could see the land in another season. That same summer, Henson discovered another tract of land located near the town of Colchester, close to the north shore of Lake Erie. This government-owned land, granted to a Mr. McCormick, was already cleared and was being rented to settlers. The group agreed that the best way to proceed would be to rent McCormick's land, farm it, and collect the proceeds so they could afford to purchase land at Dawn. In the spring of 1836, Henson and about a dozen others moved there and began to raise crops, primarily tobacco and wheat. Henson soon learned that McCormick had not complied with the stipulations of his government grant and was therefore not entitled to the rent the settlers paid him. With the aid of a lawyer, Henson appealed to the Canadian legislature for relief from the rent. He lost the first appeal, but the following year, he tried again. This time, he was successful, and they were able to continue to farm the land rent free. Because the land was owned by the government, they knew it could be sold at any time. Although they stayed and farmed the land for six or seven years, they never lost sight of their ultimate goal: to own their own land at Dawn.

In 1837 and 1838, while Henson was still farming McCormick's land grant in the Colchester area, armed rebellions against the British Crown arose in Lower and Upper Canada. The rebels were demanding an end to the status quo and the establishment of a more responsible and responsive government. Although both rebellions were put down, they did eventually lead to the unification of Lower and Upper Canada and to improved government.

During the rebellions, the fugitives from enslavement in the United States who had found a home in Canada were willing to fight to defend their new homeland. Henson said that he was put in command of the Second Essex

Company of Colored Volunteers. His name doesn't appear in military records, but the omission could be because the company was composed of volunteers, not permanent members of the military. Although it was unusual for a black man to command a military unit, there were exceptions, and Henson had already shown his ability to lead when he served as overseer on the Riley brothers' plantations.

Henson said that due to the injuries to his shoulders, he could not manage a musket, but he could wield a sword. His company, stationed at Fort Malden in Amherstburg, Ontario, guarded the Canadian border at Windsor. The Second Essex Company remained in Fort Malden from Christmas Day 1837 until the following May. On January 8, 1838, while stationed at the fort, they captured the enemy's schooner *Anne*, which transported rebels between Detroit and Windsor. The ship carried both cash and munitions, which Henson listed as "three hundred arms, two cannons, musketry, and provisions for the rebel troops."[82] The capture of the *Anne* was key to breaking up the rebellion in Upper Canada because the rebels were unable to restock provisions while the company held the fort.

Rescuing the Enslaved

When he became free, Henson vowed to help rescue others who had suffered enslavement as he had. He now began to carry out that vow. Once again, Henson would be on the Underground Railroad, this time as a conductor (guide) rather than a fugitive. He would have been aware of the perils he would face—both for returning to the land from which he had escaped and for aiding refugees—but he believed that with his "knowledge and connivance," he could help free those "groaning in captivity." If caught, he could face torture and perhaps death, he could be sold to the Deep South, and he almost certainly would never be reunited with his family. Nevertheless, he resolved to free as many as he could.

One day, when he was preaching at Fort Erie, he exhorted the people at the meeting that they had two obligations: "first, to God, for their deliverance; and then, secondly, to their fellow-men, to do all that was in their power to bring others out of bondage."[83]

After the meeting, he was approached by James Lightfoot, who had been enslaved in Kentucky and had fled to Canada five years earlier. Like most escapees, Lightfoot had come alone. He left behind his parents and seven siblings on a plantation on the banks of the Ohio River in Maysville, Kentucky. Hearing Henson's sermon, Lightfoot felt for the first time his moral obligation to free his enslaved family; he also believed that with Henson's aid, he would be able to do so.

Henson agreed to meet with Lightfoot the following week to discuss rescuing his family. At that time, he couldn't suggest any solutions, but when Lightfoot again approached him a few days later, Henson agreed to "commence the painful and dangerous task" of freeing the Lightfoot family. Henson said he left his own family in God's hands and set out on a four-hundred-mile journey on foot. When Henson reached Kentucky and found Lightfoot's family, he showed the family a token Lightfoot had given him to reassure them that he knew their son and brother. He had come to lead them to freedom, but there were complications. Lightfoot's parents were too old and lacked the endurance for a trek of hundreds of miles. His sisters had several young children, making them unsuitable for the journey, and his brothers were reluctant to leave their parents and sisters behind. An additional concern was that they would be betrayed by the excitement and the grief of their friends and family at losing them. Still, the lure of freedom was powerful, and the brothers said they would go with Henson the following year if he could return then.

Instead of heading back to Canada and safety, Henson, remembering his vow to free as many as possible, walked about fifty miles deeper into Kentucky because he had heard of a large group in Bourbon County looking for a leader to help them escape. He discovered about thirty people, some living on a plantation and some who had arrived from other locations. After spending about a week planning, Henson and the group set off. Like Henson and most escapees, they left on Saturday night—the time least likely to arouse suspicion. Henson described their grief: husbands were leaving wives, mothers were leaving children, children were leaving parents. However, had they stayed, the odds of some of them being sold were great, so one way or another, families were likely to be torn apart.

Walking at night and hiding in forests or swamps during the day, the group reached Cincinnati in three days. After a short rest, the fugitives headed to Richmond, Indiana. The city, founded by Quakers and dubbed the "Land of Promise," was an important stop on the Underground Railroad. Levi Coffin lived fewer than ten miles from Richmond. During Coffin's lifetime, as many as three thousand fugitives passed through his home, which became known as "Grand Central Station." There the fugitives found a safe home where they could rest and recuperate before they continued their journey.

Despite Richmond's role in the Underground Railroad, the area was rife with prejudice, and slave catchers were always on the lookout for runaways. Again they walked by night and hid during the day as they made their way from Richmond to Toledo, Ohio, on the shore of Lake Erie. After two weeks of traveling through the wilderness, they arrived in Toledo, a short boat ride across the lake to Canada and freedom.

On his second trip back into the United States, Henson demonstrated his skill at subterfuge. The autumn following his first foray on the Underground Railroad, he set out once more to try to bring James Lightfoot's family to Canada. After walking for about who weeks, he reached Portsmouth, Ohio, on the banks of the Ohio River. Maysville was just across the river, but he needed to wait for an afternoon ferry because he didn't want to arrive in Kentucky before dark. However, many Kentuckians in southern Ohio were suspicious of and eager to question any unfamiliar black person about his identity, his destination, and the name of his slaveholder. Henson filled a cloth with dried leaves and wrapped it around his face up to his eyes. He then pretended to be unable to talk, either from extreme toothache or mental problems. Unable to do more than mumble inarticulate sounds, the Kentuckians soon gave up trying to talk to him, and he boarded the ferry to Kentucky.

Soon after he got off the ferry, he encountered Jefferson Lightfoot, the brother of James. About six members of the family were still determined to escape, so they began making plans to leave the following Saturday night. During this interval, Henson hid in the woods during the day and met with them at night. So that their elderly parents wouldn't exhibit grief that might betray their intentions, no one told them they were leaving. To avoid being tracked by bloodhounds when they left, they found a skiff and rowed down the river so the hounds couldn't follow their scent.

During their journey from Maysville to Cincinnati, about sixty miles, they encountered several obstacles. First, their skiff sprang a leak, and they barely made it to shore. Finding a second boat slowed their progress. They were still on the river at daybreak, where they could easily be spotted and captured, so they had to go ashore and walk the last ten miles. When they were only seven miles from the city, they came to the Miami River, which was too deep to cross. After walking upstream for a mile, Henson noticed a cow and approached it. As he neared the cow, he observed it crossing the water; he had found a shallow place to ford the river. It was snowing, and the river was filled with ice. As the youngest Lightfoot was crossing, he "was seized with violent contraction of the limbs" and needed to be carried the rest of the way across. Because of all the delays, they missed their Underground Railroad connection in Cincinnati.

They were sheltered by Quakers for the night and set out again on Monday evening. The young Lightfoot who had suffered the seizure became too ill to walk, so they began carrying him on their backs and then fashioned a stretcher by tying clothes across poles. He became increasingly ill, and thinking that he would soon die, he urged the others to leave him because he was afraid that the slowness of their progress might cause the entire group to be captured. They reluctantly abandoned him, but after walking only two more miles, one of the brothers was overcome with sorrow and convinced the group to return. When they reached the young man, he appeared to be dying, but still they lifted him up and resumed their slow journey through the brush.

After all the obstacles they had faced, they encountered some good fortune. They noticed a wagon approaching, so Henson walked out onto the road and greeted the driver. By the driver's clothing and his use of the pronoun *thee*, Henson realized that the driver was a Quaker. Henson explained their situation, and the Quaker turned his wagon away from the market where he was going to sell produce, gathered the group, and headed for his home. They spent the night and were given biscuits and meat before they set out for Lake Erie the next morning. The weakened young man, the Quakers said, could stay with them until his recovery.

They knew that slave hunters would be pursuing them, so the next day they were determined to walk the forty miles to Lake Erie. Along the road, they encountered a white man walking alone. He explained that he, too, had escaped from the South. When his employers had attempted to punish him for some unnamed offense, he had fought back violently, and for his safety, his only recourse was to escape. Although Henson didn't identify the man, it's possible he was an indentured servant. Many indentured servants came from Europe to the United States to work for a specified number of years, usually seven, before being freed from their contract. Like the enslaved, many found their employment brutal and intolerable and ran away. Unlike the enslaved, however, they could more easily disappear into American and Canadian cities because of their European appearance.

The group walked all through the winter night together with the man they had met on the road. At dawn, they came to a tavern on the shore of Lake Erie. The white man woke the landlord and ordered breakfast for the group. Exhausted, they dozed off while waiting for their food. Seized by a sudden premonition, Henson demanded that all in his group leave the house and go outside, even though the snow was knee-deep. They soon heard the sound of approaching horses and hid in the brush, where they could see the front of the tavern but remain unseen. When the Lightfoots saw the horsemen, they immediately recognized them. Had they remained in the house, they would have been captured.

When the horsemen knocked on the door, their friend and fellow escapee opened the door before the tavern's landlord could. He answered their questions by saying that, yes, he had seen a group of about six black men on the road headed to Detroit and that they were probably a few miles ahead. The horsemen galloped off in the wrong direction. That man they had encountered by chance on the road had saved their lives. When the landlord learned that the men were escapees headed to Canada, he offered to take them in his boat. Henson said, "Words cannot describe the feelings experienced by my companions as they neared the shore—their bosoms were swelling with inexpressible joy as they mounted the seats of the boat, ready, eagerly, to spring forward, that they might touch the soil of the freeman. And when they reached the shore, they danced and wept for joy, and kissed the earth on which they first stepped, no longer the SLAVE—but the FREE."[84]

These two forays to rescue the enslaved via the Underground Railroad are the only ones Henson recounted in detail. He summed up his successes by saying that over time he rescued 118 people. Other sources, such as the African-American Registry, credit him with 200 rescues. Harriet Tubman, dubbed the "Black Moses," is usually said to have freed 300 of the enslaved, a number based on Sarah Bradford's 1868 biography of Tubman. But Tubman herself only claimed to have rescued about 70 people.

Because of the secrecy necessary to protect those involved in the Underground Railroad, numbers are often imprecise. What is unusual about Henson's claim of 118 is its precision. Perhaps because of his dealings in the markets, he was accustomed to keeping records. Another possibility is that the 18 in Henson's claim may have reflected his lifelong remorse for not having freed his enslaved companions years before when he led them from Isaac Riley's Maryland plantation to Amos Riley's Kentucky plantation.

Because of Henson's commitment to lead the enslaved to freedom, he repeatedly left the safety of Canada to return to the United States at his own peril—a testament to his courage and selflessness. Regardless of the exact number of people Henson freed through the Underground Railroad, he stands as one of its heroes. As Barbara Carter, Henson's great-great-granddaughter, said in a 1998 interview with the *Louisville Courier-Journal*, "Josiah Henson was another Frederick Douglass, another Harriet Tubman, another Sojourner Truth. He risked his own freedom to free others."[85]

Dawn and the British-American Institute

The stream of escapees into Upper Canada had found freedom, but they also needed to find a way to make a living. Henson said that many of those who became tenant farmers, as he had, made uninformed decisions. They would lease forested land, but by the time they had cleared the land, the lease would expire. They would have gained nothing, and the landowner would own the arable land they had created. Others planted tobacco, the only crop they were accustomed to growing. Tobacco was usually a highly profitable crop, but a glut on the market caused the price to plummet. To help remedy the poverty of the tenant farmers, and given his extensive experience managing complex plantations, Henson began to give lectures on the necessity of diversifying crops, as well on saving and investing earnings.

At this time, Henson met Hiram Wilson, who quickly became a personal friend. Charles Finney, the president of Oberlin, gave Wilson twenty-five dollars after his 1836 graduation from Oberlin Theological Seminary in Oberlin, Ohio. Finney's gift was to enable Wilson to travel to Upper Canada, observe the condition of the fugitives and assess their needs. The following year, Wilson returned to Canada, this time as a delegate of the American Anti-Slavery Society. Abolitionists were focused not only on freeing the enslaved but also on making them self-sufficient. Since Upper Canada had such a large influx of fugitives during the decades preceding the Civil War, one goal of the American Anti-Slavery Society was to help those newly freed thrive in their new country.

Wilson realized that without education, the newly freed would have little opportunity. Over the years, he established several schools, one of which—the British-American Institute—he developed with Henson. To raise funds for the new school, Wilson contacted James Canning Fuller, a Quaker friend who was an abolitionist active in the Underground Railroad. Fuller, an Englishman who lived in New York, was planning a trip to England. While there, he raised $1,500 for Wilson and Henson. To reach a consensus about the use of the funds, Wilson and Henson called a convention of black people in London, Upper Canada, in June 1838 and invited delegates from the surrounding black settlements. Henson advocated using the money to build a school. He envisioned a school that would teach the basics taught in elementary schools but would also teach the boys manual labor skills and the girls domestic skills. Adults could attend the school to develop the literacy denied them in slavery. Moreover, the school would prepare some to teach others so that they could over time "become independent of the white man

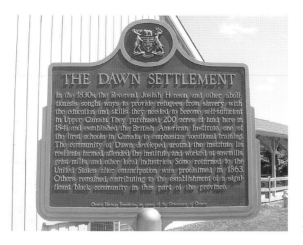

Dawn Settlement historic marker. *Ontario Plaques.*

for [their] intellectual progress."[86] After three days of discussion, Henson's proposal was approved.

The Canada Mission Board gave permission for Henson and Wilson to select a site for the school. After traveling through the area for several months, they settled on the place Henson had long thought suitable: Dawn. The area around Dawn had rich soil suitable for farming, but it also had another asset: a thick forest with a variety of hardwoods, including black walnut trees. They purchased two hundred acres at four dollars per acre. Henson personally purchased an additional two hundred acres at a discount, half of which he sold to the institute for the same low price he had paid.

On December 12, 1841, the British-American Institute opened to twelve students. Intended primarily for fugitive slaves, the school also enrolled Indians and white people. Students studied part of the day and worked part of the day. The goods produced by students were sold, with the proceeds helping to support the school. The school had six trustees: three white men, James Canning Fuller, John Roaf and Frederick Stover, and three black men, Peter Smith, George Johnson, and James C. Brown. In 1842, Henson and his family moved to Dawn.

Shortly after the school opened, Henson added a gristmill to the property. Although fugitives found freedom in Canada, they also faced considerable prejudice. Henson said that they were hindered in the everyday transactions necessary to their well-being. As an example, he told of the difficulty of getting corn ground: "A man would often walk three or four miles with two or three bushels on his shoulders, through paths in which the mud was knee-deep, leave his corn at the mill, and then go repeatedly after it in vain; he would be put off with a variety of excuses till he was quite discouraged, and would conclude that it was almost useless for him to raise any grain; and yet there was no other way for him to have a bit of bread or corn-cake."[87]

To solve the problem of gristmill owners keeping the grain brought to them by black people, Henson returned to the United States, a risky undertaking for any fugitive, and raised $5,000 from Boston philanthropists. He had a steam-powered gristmill built on the institute's land so the Dawn inhabitants had a way to grind the grain they raised.

In order to generate revenue to support the new school, Henson also built a sawmill. The usual method of clearing land in that area was to fell the trees and burn them. Henson's approach was more enterprising. The community would clear the trees, making the land suitable for farming, and use the sawmill to produce lumber, a highly marketable product, especially in the northeastern United States and England. He returned again to the United States and met with philanthropists in Boston who provided him with $1,400 for the sawmill's construction.

However, the funds he had received from Boston covered only the framework and roof of the mill. Henson again returned to Boston and explained the situation to the philanthropists, and the men endorsed a note

Reconstructed sawmill. *Photo by Edna M. Troiano.*

allowing Henson to personally borrow an additional $1,800 to complete the mill.

The sawmill, which became operational in 1845, belonged to the institute, not to Henson, but the $1,800 debt was Henson's. To pay it back, he chartered a boat, loaded it with black walnut lumber from the mill and sent it to Boston, where he sold it to Jonas Chickering, a piano manufacturer. With the sale of the lumber, he was able to pay most of his debts, but he retained some funds for future undertakings. He made several trips to the United States to sell lumber. After one lumber shipment to Boston, Henson related that when the Custom House officer gave him a bill for the duties on the sale, Henson asked if he should perhaps not pay because the Fugitive Slave Act prohibited people from any dealings with fugitives like him. The agent responded, "I have nothing to do with that.... You have acted like a man, and I deal with you as a man."[88] Henson paid but relished the incident. It seems a small thing, but for a fugitive simply to be called a man was gratifying.

Because Dawn offered a chance at both an education and employment, the settlement grew. With a sawmill, a gristmill, a blacksmith forge, a brickyard, a rope factory, shops, and a school, Dawn prospered. In 1844, the settlement was attracting the attention of abolitionists. Levi Coffin visited Dawn to see for himself the new opportunities available to refugees.

To seek funds to support the British-American Institute, Henson traveled widely throughout the northeastern United States, preaching and lecturing about the evils of slavery. During his travels, he encountered many famous people, among them the renowned poet Henry Wadsworth Longfellow. In 1842, Longfellow published *Poems on Slavery*. Although best known as the author of poems such as "Paul Revere's Ride" and "The Song of Hiawatha," Longfellow was also active in an abolitionist network that included, among other notables, Harriet Beecher Stowe, Ralph Waldo Emerson, and James Russell Lowell. On June 26, 1846, Longfellow recorded Henson's visit to his Cambridge, Massachusetts home in his diary: "In the evening Mr. Henson, a Negro, once a slave, now a preacher, called to get subscription for the school at Dawn, in Upper Canada, for education of blacks. I had a long talk with him, and he gave me an account of his escape from slavery with his family." Over the next thirty years, Longfellow contributed money to "Father Henson" many times. Longfellow's description upon meeting Henson mirrored Henry Bleby's description in *The Maimed Fugitive*: "What pleases me most in this negro is his *bonhomie*," and secondly mentioned his "crooked and stiff" right arm.[89]

At its height, Dawn's population reached nearly five hundred. However, financial difficulties plagued the British-American Institute and the Dawn settlement almost from the start. In 1845, in an attempt to stabilize the school's finances, the American Baptist Free Mission Society offered the job of secretary of the executive committee to William P. Newman, a Baptist minister in Cincinnati. Newman clashed with both Henson and Wilson and accused them of financial mismanagement—a charge they were cleared of. Newman returned to Cincinnati the following year, but he remained antagonistic toward both men.

In 1847, Hiram Wilson's wife, Hannah, who had been the school's teacher, died. Debts were mounting, and no one except Wilson had any financial credit. James Canning Fuller, the school's greatest supporter, died that same year.

There seemed to be several underlying problems. The Dawn settlement didn't generate enough revenue to hire the teachers, support the school's needs, and maintain the premises. Also, all the fugitive settlements in the area competed for revenue from outside sources, primarily white philanthropists. When the investors who had provided funds didn't see any return on their investments over the years, they became increasingly unwilling to invest in the school at Dawn.

Mismanagement was also a key problem. Henson and Wilson were both innovative, enterprising individuals, but they were not practical managers of daily affairs. Frequent charges of financial mismanagement were laid against the school, although the missing or inadequate financial records were always deemed to be due to carelessness, not to malicious intent. Although Henson was never the head of the British-American Institute, he served on its executive committee. Most of his energy, however, focused on raising funds to support the school. Henson's illiteracy may have augmented the school's management problems, as he was unable to read or write complicated documents and financial statements.

On July 19, 1848, Wilson wrote to Reverend George Whipple to inform him of the situation at Dawn. Wilson reported that at a June 10 meeting, charges of mismanagement against Henson and others were dropped. However, he urged that the school's trustees "place a benevolent & well qualified man at the head of the establishment with discretionary power." Wilson enclosed a letter from John Roaf stating that Wilson had worked "zealously & faithfully in behalf of the people of color" and that he had also accomplished what few could, but also that Wilson believed it was time for new leadership for the school and for him to devote more of his time to ministry.[90]

By 1849, the school had accrued a debt of $7,500, and at a meeting of the school's trustees and supporters, a decision was made to separate management of the school and the mill. The plan was for one party to take charge of the British-American Institute and its land and be responsible for running the school and for a second party to take charge of the mill and its land and to use the mill's profits to pay off the school's debt.

Henson said that finding someone willing to take over the school would not be difficult, but finding someone to take over the mill and be responsible for the school's debt was more challenging. Finally, Henson agreed to be responsible for the mill along with Peter Smith. Smith would attend to the daily operations of the mill, and Henson would raise funds to pay off the debt.

Wilson resigned as head of the school in 1849, citing others with weak leadership and mismanagement. However, Wilson, Henson, and the school's executive committee continued to manage the school until the American Baptist Free Mission Society agreed to take over the school's management in 1850. Reverend Samuel H. Davis, who had been pastor of the Second Baptist Church in Detroit, was brought in as the new head of school that year, and Newman returned to Canada to assist him. In 1851, William Newman took over the management of the sawmill.

The same year that Dawn was beginning to founder, the nearby Canadian settlement of Wilberforce had become less a haven for black fugitives and more a beacon for Irish immigrants fleeing the potato famine. The Oro settlement had waned since the early 1830s. But just about twenty miles south of Dawn, a new settlement was being organized. The Elgin settlement, also referred to as the Buxton Mission, was located about fifteen miles south of Chatham.

The founder of Elgin, Reverend William King, was born in Scotland in 1812, immigrated to the United States in 1833, and was ordained a Presbyterian minister in 1846. King married a Louisiana woman and became a slaveholder through inheritance upon the death of his wife and then his father-in-law. Presbyterians prohibited owning, buying, or selling the enslaved. King brought the fifteen slaves from his plantation in Louisiana to the King farm in Ohio, where he freed them. He then left them with his brother on the Ohio farm, where they were to learn skills such as farming and building. King fervently believed that emancipation was not enough: the newly freed must be provided with churches, land, education, and skills if they were to flourish. To best accomplish that, he determined to establish a settlement in Upper Canada.

In 1848, King presented a plan for the settlement to the Toronto Presbyterian Synod. The Elgin Association, named for Canada West's governor-general, James Bruce, the Eighth Lord of Elgin, was created to raise funds for the purchase of land. In 1849, the same year Dawn was in financial distress, King invited his newly freed slaves to join the new Elgin settlement, located on a tract of nine thousand acres. While the Presbyterian Church was unwilling to be responsible for the entire settlement, it did support a church and a school, together called the Buxton Mission, named for Sir Thomas Fowell Buxton, a prominent British abolitionist. Unlike the manual labor school at Dawn, the Buxton school, which opened in 1850, taught a standard classical college preparatory curriculum, including algebra, geometry, Latin, and Greek. The school was so successful that it attracted white students in the region. In 1854, the fugitive Henry Johnson said, "I left the States for Canada for rights; freedom and liberty. I came to Buxton to educate my children."[91] Because illiteracy was so prevalent among adults, King also established a night school so adults could learn to read and write.

Like Dawn, the Elgin Settlement had a sawmill and gristmill—both necessary for taming a wilderness and processing crops. By 1856, seven years after King had settled in Elgin, the town had factories, a hotel, a bank, a post office, and several shops. Three years later, as Dawn was waning, the population of Elgin had swelled to about 1,300, and by the 1860s, 2,000 people lived there.

Chapter 6

ENGLAND

THE LONDON WORLD'S FAIR

In order to raise funds for the British-American Institute, Henson started out on the first of three trips he took to England. He planned to take along some of the best black walnut boards produced at the Dawn settlement to exhibit at the 1851 London's World Fair, officially named the Great Exhibition of the Works of Industry of All Nations but referred to simply as the Crystal Palace for its location in Hyde Park. Exhibiting the walnut boards at the fair, Henson reasoned, might well lead to sales in both England and Europe, which would provide an ongoing source of revenue for the school.

As was typical of the time, Henson carried several letters of introduction with him from well-respected men in the United States and Canada. These letters enabled him to be introduced and accepted by "the very best society in the kingdom." Shortly after he arrived in England, he also began preaching. Even though his son Tom had taught him to read and write a little, Henson was still merely semiliterate; to have become such an eloquent and sought-after preacher, he must have possessed both an impressive intelligence and a prodigious memory.

Henson had not been in England long when he was confronted by the kind of infighting that dogged Dawn and other early settlements. A printed circular defamed him, reading, "That one styling himself Rev. Josiah Henson was an impostor, obtaining money under false pretenses; that he

World's Fair opening at the Crystal Palace. *Library of Congress.*

could exhibit no good credentials; that whatever money he might obtain would not be appropriated according to the wish of the donors, and that the said Josiah Henson was an artful, skillful, and eloquent man, and would probably deceive the public."[92] The three accusers were Edward Mathews, a Baptist minister, and two of the school's trustees, Samuel J. May and Hiram Wilson, the latter of whom had been Henson's friend and cofounder of the school but who had resigned his position in 1849. The accusers stated that Henson did not speak for them and had mismanaged the institute.

Meanwhile, this warning against Henson, originally published in the *American Baptist*, was widely reprinted:

> *We learn that the individual above named is in England, professing to have been sent there by the Trustees of the Dawn (C. W.) School to collect funds. The British Anti-Slavery Reporter for January says, "Mr. Henson has been sent hither to appeal to the friends of education to enable the Trustees to complete the arrangements completed some time hence." This is a mistake. Mr. Henson has no authority from the Trustees to solicit funds in England. Neither is he authorized, as we are informed, by any act of the colored refugees in Canada, to collect moneys for their aid.*[93]

The article continues by citing a resolution from a meeting of black citizens in Canada claiming that Henson had "never colonized or settled a community of Fugitive Slaves in this country" and that he "has no rightful authority to collect funds in the name of the colored people of this Province." The article concludes by exhorting "all newspapers, in this and other countries, friendly to the right, and opposed to the wrong, to publish the above resolutions."[94]

With typical foresight, Henson had previously appointed a committee of twelve to oversee his plans in England. That committee had been entrusted to appoint a subcommittee of three members and a treasurer. The subcommittee would receive the entire sum Henson raised in England and determine how the funds should be used.

Henson said that his accuser Edward Mathews was also in England at the time. A group of Henson's supporters called for the two men to meet face to face. At this encounter, Mathews repeated his charges and Henson reiterated his defense, reminding the group that "a man who devotes himself to doing good, must and will be misunderstood and have enemies."[95] The group re-read the letters of introduction, considered the charges and defense by the two men, and agreed that Henson was no impostor.

However, to clear Henson from all suspicion, the group of Englishmen decided to investigate more fully by sending John Scoble, a prominent British abolitionist, to accompany Henson back to Canada. Scoble had been selected by a London committee of philanthropists, all members of the British and Foreign Anti-Slavery Society. By this point, Henson had amassed almost $1,700, which was held, as previously decided, by the treasurer.

When Henson and Scoble arrived back in Dawn, they called a public meeting. Reverend John Roaf, one of the men who had furnished Henson with a letter of introduction, presided. Scoble and others examined all the records of the institute. Mathews denied having made the charges, and Henson was exonerated. Henson attributed the accusations that often arose in the new black settlements to slavery, saying that the enslaved were accustomed to being deceived by people who had power over them, and they maintained that suspicion once freed.

Late in 1851, Henson returned to England to display the lumber from the Dawn sawmill at the World's Fair. He had selected four black walnut boards, seven by four feet and polished so they shone like mirrors. The boards, shipped from Boston, had been carried on the same American ship that contained the American products for the exhibition. When the exhibit was mounted, Henson discovered that his boards were exhibited among the products from the United States. Henson wanted the boards to be part of the Canadian exhibit, but the superintendent of the United States exhibit refused. With typical ingenuity, Henson arranged to have a painter come to the exhibit early the next morning and paint in large, white letters, "This is the product of the industry of a Fugitive Slave from the United States, whose residence is Dawn, Canada." When the superintendent confronted him, Henson replied with feigned innocence, "Oh, that is only a little information to let the people know who I am."[96] The superintendent claimed that he had a right to the boards because he had transported them at no cost. Henson countered that he had never asked that they be brought for free and was always willing to pay. When the superintendent told Henson to remove the boards, he demurred, saying that since the superintendent had so clearly wanted the boards, he could keep them on display. Henson said the crowd that gathered obviously enjoyed the scene, although probably not more than Henson did. The boards were quickly removed to the Canadian exhibit, and Henson was never charged for their transportation to England.

Approximately 6 million people visited the Crystal Palace from May to October that year. Henson said he spoke to people from all nations and that many visitors stopped to look at him, as well as at their own images reflected in the mirror-like surface of the boards. When Queen Victoria visited the fair, she paused at his exhibit. Henson removed his hat and acknowledged the queen, who returned his greeting. He overheard her ask if he was truly a fugitive slave; she was assured not only that he was but also that the boards represented his labor.

Henson acknowledged that the visitors at the fair who stopped to look at him may have done so because he was a black man. He was not the only black person at the fair, but among all the exhibits from countries around the world, he was the only black exhibitor and therefore bound to attract attention. The other black people at the fair were *exhibits* from Africa, not exhibitors. Henson acknowledged how dramatically his life had changed from his enslaved childhood and felt saddened by the dearth of other black exhibitors, a situation he envisioned would change over time.

Henson had arrived back in England by the exhibition's close in October. He was awarded a bronze medal for the exhibit of his walnut boards, presented with a picture of Queen Victoria and her family, and given a bound volume showing all the exhibitions at the fair. Henson was pleased at the recognition he received from his exhibit, but he was also gratified to have earned enough to pay off the British-American Institute's debts.

PUBLIC LIFE

Henson was already well known in Canada, and his experiences in England made him a celebrity there as well. While in England, Henson was actively engaged in public life. The Ragged Schools were of particular interest to him. As industry developed, working-class hubs in cities became centers of extreme poverty. The Ragged Schools were a philanthropic undertaking to provide free education for destitute, inner-city children who were unable to go to traditional schools. The teachers, often local residents, found available space in their neighborhoods in places like lofts or stables. The initial curriculum included basic reading, writing, and arithmetic. Since the children were often denied participation in Sunday schools due to their appearance or behavior, religious instruction also became part of the curriculum. The Ragged Schools often added instruction in practical skills such as cooking and mending clothes, and some offered industrial skills that might eventually lead to employment. Children were in school from morning until evening and were provided with meals. In 1844, the London Ragged Schools Union was established to provide children not only with free education but also with food, clothing, lodging, and any other services they might need. An estimated 300,000 children attended Ragged Schools in London before the establishment of free public education.

Henson said that his interest in the Ragged Schools led to his visiting them and speaking at public meetings on the topic of education. Although he didn't draw the comparison, he must have felt an alliance between the efforts in London to educate the neediest and his own efforts at the British-American Institute.

England had banned slave trade in the British empire in 1807 and had abolished slavery by 1833. In speaking to English audiences, Henson depicted the ongoing atrocities of slavery in the United States, hoping to persuade the people of England to support his efforts in Canada to provide a home, employment, and education for refugees. In one public exchange, he eagerly and avidly corrected a man from Pennsylvania who claimed that all social classes in the United States were welcomed in Sunday schools.

Because of his public appearances and lectures, Henson met many famous men. Lord Grey, who had served as prime minister from 1830 to 1834, offered Henson the opportunity to go to India to oversee the cultivation of cotton because Henson could apply his knowledge of cotton farming in the southern United States. Although the offer appealed to Henson, he declined because of his dedication to the enterprises in Dawn.

One of the highlights of Henson's time in England was meeting John Bird Sumner, the archbishop of Canterbury. Philanthropist Samuel Gurney sent a note of introduction to the archbishop, who invited Henson to visit. After a half hour's conversation, the archbishop asked Henson what university he had graduated from. When Henson replied, the "University of Adversity," the archbishop was astonished that a man, born enslaved with no formal education, could speak so eloquently. Henson recounted his efforts, which began when he was in the marketplaces in Montgomery County, Georgetown, and Washington, D.C., and continued through the years, to listen to and model the speech of other well-spoken, well-educated men. Archbishop Sumner was equally surprised that a man brought up without religious instruction could become the widely admired preacher Father Henson. Henson gave tribute to his mother, who taught him the Lord's Prayer, and to his conversion upon hearing his first sermon, where he learned that "He, by the grace of God, tasted death for every man." Archbishop Sumner invited Henson to visit again and contributed fifty pounds sterling for Henson's enterprises.

Henson said that one of the most pleasant days of his life was in June 1852, when he, along with a group of about three hundred Sunday school teachers, met Lord John Russell, prime minister of England. Henson described the prime minister's grounds as "filled with deer, of varied colours, from all climes, and sleek hares, which the poet Cowper would have envied, with numberless birds, whose plumage rivalled the rainbow in gorgeous colours, together with the choicest specimens of the finny tribe, sporting in their native element."[97] He then contrasted the park to the dismal condition of those still enslaved in the United States. After a picnic on the grounds, the group was ushered into Lord Russell's mansion, where they were treated to a sumptuous banquet with Henson in the place of honor at the head of the table. For a man who had faced hunger and given his thirsty children a drink of water out of his shoes, the contrast must have seemed astounding.

During this second trip to England, he had met three of the nation's most distinguished citizens: the archbishop of Canterbury, a former prime minister, and the current prime minister. During his third visit, he would meet the most distinguished: Queen Victoria.

Chapter 7

RETURN TO CANADA

Called Home

In June and July 1852, Henson wrapped up his work in England and prepared to close his agency there. The month of August he devoted to his second autobiography. In the title of his first autobiography, he had described himself as "formerly a slave." This second autobiography was titled *Truth Stranger than Fiction: Father Henson's Story of His Own Life*, adding his role as a pastor to the amazing story of his life.

On September 3, Henson received a letter saying that his wife, Charlotte, was gravely ill and wanted to see him once again before she died. Less than a day later, he was on his way from London to Liverpool, where he would catch a steamer to Boston the following day. He arrived in Dawn on September 20. In his angst and uncertainty, he said, "I knew not whether my dear wife, the mother of my children, she who had travelled with me, sad, solitary, and footsore, from the land of bondage, who had been to me a kind, affectionate, and dutiful wife for forty years, was still alive, or whether she had entered into her rest." Charlotte survived for a few more weeks, with Henson by her side day and night. Henson described her death: "She blessed me, and blessed her children, commending us to the ever-watchful care of that Saviour who had sustained her in so many hours of trial; and finally, after kissing me and each one of her children, she passed from earth to heaven without a pang or a groan, as gently as the falling to sleep of an

Josiah and Nancy Henson. *Uncle Tom's Cabin Historic Site.*

infant on its mother's breast."[98] Henson was bereft after Charlotte's death: "My heart and home were desolate after I lost the wife who had been my faithful companion in slavery, and had escaped with me to Canada."[99]

After grieving for Charlotte for four years, Henson realized how lonely he was and decided to remarry. Although he was acquainted with many women through his travels, only one appealed to him: Boston widow Nancy Gamble. Her mother had been a slave but had been able to purchase her own and her husband's freedom. Nancy was an educated woman who was active in her church and taught in the Sunday school. The couple were married by a bishop in Boston. Toward the end of his life, Henson said of Nancy, "She has made me an excellent wife, and my cup has indeed run over with God's mercies."[100]

Ransoming His Brother

Before his visit to England, Henson had made several attempts to free his brother John, who was enslaved at the Beall-Dawson House in Montgomery County, Maryland, just a few miles from where Henson had worked at Isaac Riley's plantation. It's unclear when John Henson came to the Beall family, but it could have been as early as 1805, at the auction when Henson's mother was sold to Isaac Riley and Josiah was sold to Adam Robb.

The Beall family were some of the largest owners of enslaved workers in Montgomery County. The Beall house was built by Upton Beall circa 1815. Upon his death in 1827, he owned twenty-five enslaved workers. Upon their mother's death, the Beall daughters inherited forty enslaved, a number that increased to fifty-two by the 1860 census. The daughters neither bought nor sold enslaved persons, so the increase must have been due to births in the enslaved community. There is one exception to their refusal to buy or sell the enslaved: they agreed to sell John Henson to his brother Josiah.

Even though Henson had twice sent William Lawrence Chaplin, a prominent New York abolitionist, to convince his brother John to escape via the Underground Railroad, John had refused. Henson attributed his brother's refusal to flee to a mind "demoralized or stultified by slavery." John, however, said he was unwilling to "risk his life in the attempt to gain his freedom."

Chaplin, unable to persuade John to leave, tried instead to help a man and a woman from Georgia escape. The group was captured by slave catchers.

Chaplin was beaten and jailed prior to trial. His bail was paid by abolitionists, who encouraged him to escape rather than face a trial that might well lead to his being hanged.

While still in England, Henson had determined that despite Chaplin's failed attempts, he would free his brother after his return to Canada. Since he couldn't persuade him to escape, he decided to buy his freedom. Henson learned that John's slaveholder would sell him for $400, so Henson estimated he would need about $550 to free his brother and bring him to Dawn. Through negotiations by a Boston banker, the cost of John's freedom was reduced to $250.

To raise the funds to ransom his brother, Henson contacted abolitionist friends in Boston, and they agreed to publish his life story, which he had completed just prior to returning to Canada. Stowing the books on his back, Henson traveled through New England, selling them along the way until he had raised enough money to ransom his brother. He sent the required funds through a Boston bank, and his brother John then traveled from Baltimore to Boston, where he met Josiah. They returned together to Dawn, and John resided with the Henson family for the next fifteen years.

John Henson's eldest son lived in New Jersey, where his family worked as hired labor on a large dairy farm. Three years after the Emancipation Proclamation, the son traveled to Dawn to take his father to New Jersey with him. On the dairy farm, John's son explained, the family earned "excellent wages for their faithful service," making a clear distinction from the work the enslaved had performed without compensation before emancipation.

The Demise of the British-American Institute

In 1842, the British and Foreign Anti-Slavery Society, concerned about mismanagement, had taken over the management of the British-American Institute. In 1852, John Scoble, who had previously traveled to Canada to investigate the accusations against Henson, was entrusted with the management of the school. Scoble, born in 1799 in England, had been active in England's antislavery movement. He had taken part in an investigation of the apprenticeship program that had replaced slavery in the West Indies. Scoble's finding that the apprenticeship program violated the 1833 Emancipation Act led to the closing down of that program. A charter member of the British and Foreign Anti-Slavery Society, established in 1838,

Scoble served as its secretary from 1842 to 1852. During that period, he was involved in three world antislavery conferences and was responsible for reorganizing the French antislavery movement. Scoble seemed an ideal candidate to stabilize and manage the British-American Institute.

Henson approved of Scoble as the new manager of the British-American Institute; in fact, he said he had "great faith in him." He knew of Scoble's reputation as an abolitionist and of his work in the West Indies, and he had previously benefited personally from Scoble's defense of him against his accusers. Henson quoted Scoble as saying that the British-American Institute "could be made the brightest spot in the garden of the Lord, if there were only an efficient manager at its head to control it." Scoble further promised to eliminate the school's debt and said that the committee in London, selected by Henson, "would aid him in placing the school on a permanent foundation, and in making it a glorious moral lighthouse, a beacon whose illumination should be perpetual."[101] Henson was particularly thrilled by Scoble's promise to completely renovate the school building. However, Scoble had one caveat: the trustees of the British-American Institute must relinquish their control to him.

Scoble, despite his achievements as an abolitionist, was not without detractors. On July 2, 1852, *The Liberator*, having learned that Scoble was to accompany Henson to Canada to take charge of the school at Dawn, warned readers, "It will be well for the Abolitionists to watch well the course of a man in Canada, who, like Mr. Scoble, has been the constant villifier and systematic opponent of the most devoted friends of the Slave on your side of the water. It is to be hoped he will not instil any of his anti-slavery notions into the Canadian community, they having done mischief enough in this country." The article concluded by describing Scoble as a man "whose malignity of spirit is equaled only by its meanness and unscrupulousness."[102]

The Canadian trustees (with the exception of James C. Brown, who remained adamantly opposed) agreed to cede their responsibility for the institute to a London committee. Since the British-American Institute always struggled financially, an attempt was made to incorporate the institute in Canada in order to eliminate personal liability if the financial situation was untenable and the school had to declare bankruptcy. The goal was to prevent a recurrence of the situation when Henson took on the school's debt and then toured to raise money. The attempt to incorporate the institute in Canada failed.

Scoble was never successful in his Canadian endeavors. Henson said that it was his "candid opinion that, in the beginning, he intended to benefit the couloured race, and to have a splendid school which should be the pride of the neighborhood. If he had been a practical instead of a theoretical farmer, he doubtless would have accomplished those blessed results."[103] The American Baptist Free Mission Society had become tenants of the land from 1851 to 1853; it also quarreled with Scoble. In 1853, agents of the Baptist Free Mission Society removed everything that was portable from the land.

The school, now dilapidated, was closed in 1852. From Scoble's point of view, his inability to construct new buildings and put the school on solid financial footing was due to squabbles between the original trustees—especially James C. Brown—and the new trustees. Henson's view was that Scoble made impractical choices:

> *He soon began to buy the most expensive cattle in the market, at fancy prices, and without any reference to the fact that he had not sufficient fodder to feed them after he had them in his stables. He also bought expensive farming utensils to work the farm scientifically, and then pulled down the school-buildings, as they were too primitive to suit his magnificent ideas, and he promised to erect more substantial and commodious buildings. I upheld him in all these suggestions, for I had a kind of respect for the man that almost amounted to veneration.*[104]

An inherent problem for the British-American Institute was that the it was never able to generate enough revenue to support itself. The cost of clearing land and developing the settlement, compounded by infighting among trustees and tenants on the land, left little support available for the institute. Scoble exacerbated the problem with his failure to rebuild the school. Finally, Henson confronted Scoble, telling him that people were angered by his inaction. Scoble replied, "I did not come here for the coloured people to dictate to me." At this point, Henson said, "The scales fell from my eyes."[105]

Henson admitted to the people that he had been badly deceived. The only way to rebuild the school, he concluded, was for the people of the community to regain ownership of the land. After meeting with and securing permission from the local community, Henson consulted two lawyers from London, Ontario. Because Henson clearly had a conflict of interest, the lawyers agreed to take the case if someone else served as plaintiff. James C. Brown, who had remained at odds with Scoble throughout the years, agreed to sue Scoble for "non-fulfillment of trusts and for maladministration of the affairs of the school." Henson, who agreed to pay the costs of the suit, incurred significant debts. The lawsuits dragged on for seven years. He said that he first "paid two hundred dollars, and borrowed money from time to time by mortgaging, first one house and lot, then three houses and lots, then re-mortgaging them, then sold several lots to pay the mortgages, then re-mortgaged, and was constantly called upon to pay disbursements to the lawyers."[106] Finally, in 1868, Scoble's lawyer agreed to abandon the efforts if his expenses during the seven years could be paid, after which, Henson said, the case was decided in his favor.

Like the British-American Institute, the sawmill suffered from poor management. Henson said the sawmill had several years of prosperity under his and then Newman's management. Scoble appointed a new manager, whom Henson did not name, and the mill began to founder. The manager, after filling and launching three ships with timber, disappeared. The mill workers remained unpaid for their labor. When they realized that he did not intend to return, they dismantled the entire mill, tearing up even the foundations. The loss of the sawmill was also the loss of any potential revenue through lumber sales to salvage the British-American Institute and the Dawn community.

When the lawsuit against Scoble began, Henson decided to sell the gristmill. He personally owned it, but it was located on the institute's land, so he needed to move it. The simplest method was through subterfuge: Henson's son-in-law was the miller, and he and Henson arranged for twenty men to hide in the mill on a Sunday night. At midnight, they disassembled the entire mill and removed it from the institute's premises. The next morning, by prearrangement, the mill was moved by about a dozen teams to the nearby town of Dresden, where it was reassembled. Once again, Henson had accomplished his goal through connivance, a skill that had repeatedly served him well.

Scoble left the institute after he resigned his trusteeship in 1861, leaving his son in charge of the land. Henson had rented a portion of the land and had farmed it for several years when, one day, Scoble's son appeared and told Henson's men to get off the land. Henson told his men to return in the morning and resume plowing. Henson joined them and told the young Scoble, "I leased this land from your father, and as long as he retains the possession of the whole farm I have a legal right to work this plot, and I shall defend that right." Clearly miscalculating Henson's character, Scoble's son said, "Why, Mr. Henson, is that you? I thought you were a praying man, not a fighting man." Henson replied, "When it is necessary, I can fight, as I have done for Canada when she was in trouble."

The quarrel escalated, Henson said, from words to blows. With his typical sense of humor, Henson noted, "I could not prevent him from bruising his head several times against my heavy walking-stick, which I held before me to ward off the blows he attempted to level at me." The son intended to see his father and have charges leveled against Henson. But Henson went to the nearest magistrate as quickly as possible, leveled charges and brought a constable who said to Scoble, "You are my prisoner, in the name of the Queen, for assault and battery on Josiah Henson on his own premises."[107] The trial moved from site to site until young Scoble ended the trial by paying costs and a bonus. Henson pointed out that this incident illustrates the importance of fugitives having a basic understanding of the law in order to protect their rights once they became Canadian citizens.

With Scoble no longer in control, a new board was established. In 1872, the trustees agreed to sell the school and the land. After the remaining debts were cleared, the assets from the sale were used to support the Wilberforce Educational Institute in Chatham. The British-American Institute had struggled with debt from its beginning. Despite recurrent charges against Henson as unfit and as having mismanaged the institute, no one ever accused him of doing so for personal gain: his devotion to the Dawn Settlement and the British-American Institute was unwavering. Henson was nearly illiterate, and no one else, including Wilson, Davis, and Scoble—all of whom had formal education—was able to successfully manage the institute either.

Henson had envisioned the Dawn Settlement and the British-American Institute and worked tirelessly to create and support them. He was the community's acknowledged patriarch and its religious leader, and he served on the institute's executive committee. But he was never the administrative head of the school. Hiram Wilson served in that capacity from the institute's 1842 opening to his resignation in 1849. A subsequent attempt to rule by committee was unsuccessful, and from 1850 to 1852, Samuel H. Davis, a member of the American Baptist Free Mission Society, served in that role. Davis was replaced by Scoble from 1852 to 1861. Despite Henson's dream of a community by and for black refugees, the two long-term heads of the school—Wilson and Scoble—were white.

During those turbulent years at Dawn, Henson continued to be active in the abolitionist cause. Although united in the cause of abolition and in improving the lives of the formerly enslaved, abolitionists differed vehemently in their approaches. Frederick Douglass (1818–1895), who like Henson had been enslaved in Maryland, and William Lloyd Garrison (1805–1879) became two of the foremost abolitionists in the

United States. Initially, both men believed in the power of moral suasion, the idea that if people understood the atrocity of slavery, they would be persuaded, on moral grounds, to support abolition. Gradually, both men veered in different directions. Douglass, who believed in the power of politics to bring about social change, began to endorse violence as a solution, encouraging revolts by the enslaved and supporting John Brown's raid at Harper's Ferry in 1859. Garrison also abandoned the notion that moral suasion was enough to prompt abolition and gradually moved from expecting gradual improvement to demanding immediate emancipation.

Both Douglass and Garrison were literate men who used the power of the news media, Douglass through the *North Star* and Garrison through *The Liberator*. Unlike Douglass and Garrison, Henson was semiliterate and lacked the large audience they attracted through their newspapers.

Henson was, however, well known throughout Canada, the northeast United States, and England and promoted his views widely in meetings and through sermons and lectures. In August 1858, he attended the Convention of the Colored Citizens of Massachusetts in New Bedford, Massachusetts. At that meeting, Henson advocated that enslaved people escape to Canada as he had, stating that "a good run was better than a bad stand." Massachusetts abolitionist Charles Remond, although he knew his proposal would not be endorsed, proposed establishing a committee to write an address urging the enslaved in the South to "rise with bowie-knife, revolver, and musket." Henson, having quelled an uprising at Amos Riley's plantation in 1829 and seen the results of Nat Turner's uprising, vehemently opposed the idea, responding that "he didn't want to see three or four thousand men hung before their time." He added that circulating such a document in the South was not feasible and that the enslaved "had nothing to fight with—no weapons, no education." Furthermore, Henson added, "When I fight, I want to whip somebody."[108]

A few decades may seem a short period of time for a community to be built and then decline, but Oro, Wilberforce, and Elgin thrived no longer than that as well. These communities were not failures; they simply outlived their purpose. All the black Canadian settlements had met a crucial need for the fugitives who needed land, housing, education, and employment. But they were not utopias; although the settlers were free, they faced the same prejudices that beset black people in the United States. Most of the fugitives turned to farming, the only experience they had when enslaved, but they were now in a less hospitable climate for agriculture than they had been accustomed to. Furthermore, to gain freedom, most of them had been separated from family and friends. Once the Civil War began, many of the inhabitants of the area returned to the United States, some to enlist in the Union army. Upon emancipation, many more returned to the United States to reunite with families or return to a more familiar culture. Henson, however, remained in Canada, living with his family in Dresden until his death in 1883.

Chapter 8

UNCLE TOM

UNCLE TOM'S CABIN

On June 5, 1851, the *National Era*, an antislavery weekly paper in Washington, published the first installment of Harriet Beecher Stowe's novel *Uncle Tom's Cabin; or, Life Among the Lowly*. The serial continued until April of the following year, and just over a week before the last installment was to appear, the entire novel was published in two volumes on March 20, 1852, by John P. Jewett and Company. The novel was a publishing phenomenon. In the first year, 300,000 copies were sold in the United States, and about 1.5 million copies sold in England over the next few years. The blockbuster novel was translated into several languages and became the bestselling novel of the nineteenth century. President Abraham Lincoln was even purported to have said, upon meeting Stowe, "So you're the little woman who wrote the book that started this great war." Although the quotation is probably apocryphal, it illustrates the novel's impact on culture and politics. To many readers, the sentimental, melodramatic novel now seems dated both in form and content; however, it remains for literary critics an example of the power of literature to transform society.

Despite the phenomenal sales, the novel was loathed as well as loved. Langston Hughes, one of the great poets of the Harlem Renaissance, called it "the most cussed and discussed book of its time." The novel depicts the evils of slavery by showing both the atrocities endured by the enslaved as well as the deleterious effects of slavery on slaveholders. Slaveholders

Cover of *Uncle Tom's Cabin*. *Uncle Tom's Cabin Historic Site.*

argued that Stowe's depiction was wildly skewed and that slavery was a far more benign institution than the one she depicted. They also assumed that a woman who was an ardent abolitionist from a large family of social activists was bound to be inherently biased. The anti–Uncle Tom rhetoric was pervasive in the South; in fact, schoolchildren in Virginia and in Kentucky were taught to sing this song: "Go, go, go, / Ol' Harriet Beecher Stowe! / We don't want you in Kentucky, / So go, go, go!"

Most reactions against Stowe's novel were not as innocuous as the children's song. Slaveholders and those who deemed slavery an economic necessity endorsed by the Bible vehemently denounced Stowe in sermons, newspaper articles, and letters. In addition to being the subject of widespread public scorn, Stowe received threatening letters, and once she was even mailed a box containing a severed black ear.

As an abolitionist, Stowe's purpose was to illustrate the evils of slavery and to do so in a manner designed to evoke strong emotions among her readers. The argument by proslavery advocates that a northerner couldn't understand slavery was belied by the extensive reading she did and the conversations she had with slaves and fugitives, including a meeting with Josiah Henson.

The novel intertwines two plots, one ending in freedom and happiness and the other in bondage and death. Uncle Tom, a hardworking, pious man who has been promised his freedom, is the most valuable worker on the Shelby plantation in Kentucky. Nevertheless, he is to be sold along with Harry, a four-year-old boy, to pay the family debts that have accrued through carelessness. Harry's mother, Eliza, who has been promised that her son will never be sold, overhears a conversation and learns that Haley, a slave trader, has bought Harry and is coming for him the following day. She is determined to escape with him. Her husband, George Harris, badly abused by his slaveholder, has said farewell to Eliza, saying he intends to escape to Canada. Eliza hopes to join him there. Pursued by Haley, Eliza makes a daring escape, clutching her son as she leaps from one chunk of ice to another

Eliza escaping across the river.
Library of Congress.

until she reaches the other side of the Ohio River. Tom, however, refuses to escape: he agrees to be sold because the money his sale brings will prevent Mr. Shelby from selling other slaves. He sacrifices himself in the hope that the family will buy him back as soon as possible, as Mrs. Shelby has promised.

Having made it across the raging river, Eliza and Harry are helped up the banks of the river and taken to a Quaker settlement. By coincidence, George meets his wife and son at the settlement, and the family, with two other fugitives, sets out for Canada. The slave trader Haley hires Loker and his helper, Marks, to pursue Eliza and Harry and bring them back. At one point, the fugitives are trapped among some rocks, but George saves them by shooting Loker, which causes the other slave hunters to retreat and scatter. In an act of compassion, Eliza, George, and the Quakers who accompany them decide to bring Loker to the next Quaker settlement so he can heal from his gunshot wound.

Loker's experience with the Quakers who care for him in his illness changes him. He says that although the Quakers were unable to convert him, he did give up slave hunting and turned to hunting in nature, making his living from animals, not people. He even sends a warning to the Harris family that slave hunters are looking for them. Eliza cuts her hair and disguises herself as a man, and little Harry is dressed as a girl. In disguise, they make their way to freedom in Canada.

Tom's experience does not echo the happy ending of the Harris family. Despite the Shelby family's repeated promises that they would free him, he is led off in shackles by Loker to be taken by boat down the Mississippi to a New Orleans slave market. On the boat, Tom encounters a charming little white girl, Evangeline, whose name implies both *angel* and *evangelist*. Eva befriends Tom, and when Eva falls off the boat, Tom unhesitatingly leaps into the river and saves her. At Eva's insistence, her father, Augustine St. Clare, buys Tom.

Augustine St. Clare is a wealthy Louisiana planter, easygoing, kind, and generous. Although St. Clare's conscience is troubled by slavery, he does not act to free his slaves or advance abolition in any way. His wife, Marie, is his antithesis—a hardened, self-obsessed hypochondriac who has no concern for the enslaved. Since Marie often suffers from undefined illnesses, St. Clare brings his cousin Ophelia to help with the household. Ophelia is a New Englander who abhors the institution of slavery yet still harbors a deep-set prejudice against black people.

At the St. Clare home, Tom and Eva's friendship grows deeper. The two are bound by their devout Christianity. After about two years, Eva becomes ill with what the reader likely infers is tuberculosis. Meanwhile, St. Clare buys a little girl, Topsy, for Ophelia, causing her to confront her bigotry as she tries to tame and educate the unmanageable child.

Eva's death, devastating to everyone, causes profound changes in some of the characters. Ophelia learns to genuinely love Topsy, who in turn learns to trust others and become the person Eva had urged her to be. St. Clare is moved by his daughter's religious fervor and decides he must free Tom. Having told Tom of his intentions, St. Clare goes to a café. A fight erupts, and when St. Clare tries to separate the two brawling men, he is stabbed.

St. Clare is brought home to die. First Shelby and now St. Clare have promised Tom his freedom. Instead of freeing Tom, Marie St. Clare, indifferent to all suffering except her own imagined illnesses, has St. Clare's slaves taken to a New Orleans slave pen. Tom is among the enslaved bought by Simon Legree, a cruel, depraved owner of a dilapidated cotton plantation in rural Louisiana. Another of Legree's purchases is a young woman named Emmeline, whom Legree intends to use as a sex slave to replace Cassy, his current sex slave.

On the way to the plantation, Legree has Tom dress in the coarsest of clothes and takes ownership of Tom's clothes and all his possessions except for his Bible. Infuriated by Tom's fervent religious beliefs, Legree swears to rid Tom of all religion, saying, "I'm your church now!"

In the cotton field, Tom works hard and helps weaker workers fill their sacks to reach the requisite weight for the day's pick. When Legree orders Tom to flog a woman he falsely accuses of not having picked enough cotton, Tom refuses. Legree whips and kicks Tom before turning him over to two of his thugs, who beat Tom brutally. Near death, Tom lies in a shed, where at night Cassy brings him water. The next day, Legree tells Tom to apologize, but he refuses, saying he did the right thing. Legree threatens to kill Tom, but since he needs every hand in the field, he walks away. In the midst of despair, Tom has a vision of heaven.

Cassy gives Tom a chance at freedom. One night, she slips extra brandy into Legree's drink so that he sleeps soundly. Then she unlocks the back

Simon Legree beating Tom. *Library of Congress.*

door, leaving an axe beside it. All Tom has to do is enter the house and wield the axe, and he and others will be free. Tom refuses on Christian principle and also dissuades Cassy from committing murder.

Cassy and Emmeline concoct an elaborate plan to convince the superstitious Legree that he has seen their ghosts. The two women escape, and when Tom refuses to tell Legree where they have gone, he is beaten again. Near death, Tom forgives Legree and the overseers who have repeatedly beaten him.

George Shelby, the son of Tom's original slaveholder, arrives at Legree's plantation, intent on purchasing Tom and returning him to the Kentucky plantation. George finds Tom, who welcomes death and eagerly awaits heaven. Later in life, after his father has died, George frees all the slaves on his plantation.

Cassy and Emmeline, disguised as a Creole Spanish lady and her maid, board a boat on the Mississippi and head north toward Canada. On board, they encounter a woman who turns out to be George Harris's sister. When they reach Canada, Cassy discovers that Eliza Harris is her daughter, sold from her in childhood. The family is reunited in Canada. The family first travels to France and then settles in Liberia, an African colony founded for the former American enslaved.

BECOMING UNCLE TOM

When Henson published his second autobiography, he added "Father Henson" to the book's title because he had become famous for his preaching in the United States, Canada, and England. In the third and fourth versions of his life story, he added another attribution, "Uncle Tom," to the titles. The fourth iteration of his autobiography was titled *Autobiography of Josiah Henson: An Inspiration for Harriet Beecher Stowe's Uncle Tom's Cabin.*

A review of the plot makes it seem strange that Josiah Henson—a man who escaped slavery, saved others through the Underground Railroad, and founded a school and a settlement for fugitives—would be conflated with Uncle Tom, a man who was "sold down the river," worked on a cotton plantation and died from repeated beatings.

The initial inspiration for the novel, Stowe admitted, was not based on any person; it was religious. Stowe said that several months prior to publishing the first installment, while taking communion in church, she envisioned an enslaved man, a devout Christian, praying on his deathbed for those who were beating him to death. Students of literature recognize Uncle Tom as a literary archetype, the Christ figure. Like Christ, Uncle Tom sacrifices himself so others will be saved, first when he agrees to be sold so that others will not be and again at the novel's end when he is willing to die rather than betray Cassy and Emmeline. He talks to other characters about God and prays they will become believers. Finally, as he is being tortured to death, he prays for and forgives his enemies.

Nevertheless, Stowe did base some of her characters on real people. The scene early in the novel in which Eliza, clutching her young son, flees from Kentucky across the Ohio River, leaping barefoot from one chunk of ice in the raging river to another until she arrives at the opposite bank, seems preposterous. Yet Stowe said that she knew Eliza and her husband, George, and had spoken with the man who helped Eliza up the riverbank and led her to safety. Henson said that he knew the couple well during their time in Canada. And the renowned

Harriet Beecher Stowe. *Uncle Tom's Cabin Historic Site.*

Levi Coffin told the story of Eliza crossing the Ohio in his *Reminiscences of Levi Coffin*, having heard of it from Eliza herself.

Knowing that the characters of Eliza, Harry, and George were based on real people, it was inevitable that readers of *Uncle Tom's Cabin* would start looking for other people behind the novel's characters. Part of the search was fueled by curiosity—readers were convinced they knew a man just like St. Clare or a little girl as angelic as Eva. The impetus for abolitionists was that their cause would be strengthened if they could demonstrate that the novel was based on real people, thus proving that Stowe had not exaggerated the atrocities of slavery.

In 1853, in response to accusations by outraged proslavery advocates that her novel was preposterous and also to widespread public curiosity about the people behind the characters, Stowe published *A Key to Uncle Tom's Cabin: Presenting the Original Facts and Documents Upon Which the Story Is Founded*. At the beginning of the key, she explained the relationship between fact and fiction in her novel:

> At different times, doubt has been expressed whether the representations of "Uncle Tom's Cabin" are a fair representation of slavery as it at present exists. This work, more, perhaps, than any other work of fiction that ever was written, has been a collection and arrangement of real incidents—of actions really performed, of words and expressions really uttered—grouped together with reference to a general result, in the same manner that the mosaic artist groups his fragments of various stones into one general picture. His is a mosaic of gems—this is a mosaic of facts.[109]

In the *Key*, Stowe acknowledged multiple sources, including numerous contacts and conversations with fugitives, abolitionists, and the enslaved. She acknowledged reading Henson's first memoir. She may also have heard about his life from the many people she spoke to as she gathered information for *Uncle Tom's Cabin*. But she also acknowledged additional sources. Stowe said that she kept Theodore Dwight Weld's compilation, *American Slavery as It Is: Testimony of a Thousand Witnesses*, close by her as she wrote. In addition, she noted the parallels between her novel and Solomon Northup's memoir, *Twelve Years a Slave*.

Those characters who are fictional—Stowe begins with the slave trader Haley and Mr. and Mrs. Shelby—exemplify a type of person, in this case the callous slave trader and the generally benevolent and good slaveholder. Miss Ophelia represents "a numerous class of the very best of Northern people" who are antislavery yet remain prejudiced against black people.[110] Even when characters are fictional, Stowe provided solid evidence of the accuracy of her portrayals based on meetings with people and reading of documents.

Of Henson, Stowe said, "The character of Uncle Tom has been objected to as improbable; and yet the writer has received more confirmations of that character, and from a greater variety of sources, than any other in the book. Many people have said to her, 'I knew an Uncle Tom in such and such a Southern State.' All the histories of this kind which have thus been related to her would of themselves, if collected, make a small volume."[111] After giving several examples of men who shared the values of Uncle Tom, she concluded that "[a] last instance parallel with that of Uncle Tom is to be found in the published memoirs of the venerable Josiah Henson."[112] That Stowe had many models for Uncle Tom strengthens her abolitionist argument: many of the enslaved were intelligent, strong, devout, honorable, and deserving of freedom.

Like others who were eager to find the real people behind the fictional characters, Henson believed he could identify several, including Topsy, St. Clare, Eva, and Simon Legree. On the Riley plantation in Kentucky, he knew a young girl named Dinah who he says "was clear-witted, as sharp and cunning as a fox, but she purposely acted like a fool, or idiot, in order to take advantage of her mistress." Her behavior, Henson explained, was to her advantage: "She was so queer and funny in her ways, that she was constantly doing all kinds of odd things, but escaped the whipping that other slaves, who did not behave half so badly, had received daily, because her mistress thought she was an idiot."[113]

Henson further identified Mr. St. Clair Young, who lived near the Kentucky plantation, as the possible model for Stowe's St. Clare because of his kindhearted nature and added that his "sweet little girl" daughter resembled "precious little Eva."

While Henson refrained from saying that Bryce Litton, the overseer who attacked and maimed him, was the model for Simon Legree, he did say the two were equal in character and behavior:

> *Bryce Litton, who broke my arm and maimed me for life, would stand well for Mrs. Stowe's cruel Legree. Litton was the most tyrannical, barbarous man I ever saw, and I have good reason to know that his revengeful and malicious spirit would have led him to perform the most cruel acts. He lived a miserable life, like a hog, and died like a dog a few*

years after I left that part of the country. He was universally detested even among slaveholders, for when an overseer far exceeded the bounds of what they termed humanity, he was a marked man, his society was avoided, and his career was by no means a pleasant one. Even slaveholders, like thieves, had a certain code of honor.[114]

Henson's identification of the people he believed to be depicted by fictional characters encouraged readers to believe that he must be among them. Although Henson did not claim to be Uncle Tom, he referred to Stowe's remarks on his autobiography, saying, "If my humble words in any way inspired that gifted lady to write such a plaintive story...I have not lived in vain; for I believe that her book was the beginning of the glorious end."[115] Henson summed up his discussion of the characters in *Uncle Tom's Cabin* by saying that the novel does not exaggerate the evils of slavery; in fact, the unvarnished truth about slavery "would be too horrible to hear."[116]

The curiosity about the people behind the characters persisted for decades. In a letter written on July 27, 1882, Stowe replied to a request for information from the *Indianapolis Times* about the inspiration for the character of Uncle Tom. Stowe again explained that her character was not based on any one individual. Stowe's cook had told her about her husband, enslaved in Kentucky, who was entrusted to sell produce in Cincinnati, where he could have declared his freedom. However, he had promised his slaveholder that as a Christian he would keep his word to return from Ohio. Four or five years later, Stowe said, she "conceived the plan to write a history about a faithful Christian slave." She noted that after she began writing the novel, she came across Henson's autobiography in the reading rooms of the Massachusetts Anti-Slavery Society in Boston and "included some of its most striking incidents" in the novel.[117]

Despite the stark differences in the life of Josiah Henson and Uncle Tom, there are compelling similarities:

- Both are enslaved in plantations in Kentucky.
- Both Josiah and Tom are farm managers who have the complete trust of their slave owners (*Uncle Tom's Cabin*, 42).
- Both are converted at meetings and remain pious throughout their lives.
- Both are trusted to go to Ohio, a free state, and return with large sums of money (*UTC*, 43).
- Both are sold to cover debts, Josiah as a child and Tom as an adult.

- Both are respected and acknowledged as religious leaders in their communities and are referred to as preachers in their Kentucky communities (*UTC*, 79).
- Henson is led to believe he can buy his freedom; Tom is promised his freedom by Shelby (*UTC*, 82).
- Both men vow to never break their word, which they attribute to their faith (*UTC*, 112).
- When faced with difficulties, both men repeatedly say they put their trust in God.
- Both men are taken down the Mississippi to be sold at slave auctions in New Orleans.
- Tom saves Eva from drowning; Henson recalled saving a little girl named Susan from drowning in Blackford Creek on Amos Riley's plantation.
- Both men have the opportunity to kill the man who endangers them with a conveniently placed axe, and both refuse on Christian principles.
- Henson loved his slaveholder's son, Frank; Tom loves his slaveholder's son, George.
- Both men remain good natured despite being beaten, cheated, and sold.
- Both men admit to being proud of their honesty (*UTC*, 194).
- Both men are taught to read haltingly late in life (*UTC*, 229), Henson by his eldest son and Uncle Tom by his slaveholder's son (*UTC*, 68–69).
- Uncle Tom has charge of all the marketing and attendant finances for the St. Clare family (*UTC*, 305), just as Henson had for Isaac and Amos Riley.
- Both men pity their slaveholder, Tom for St. Clare's lack of religious belief (*UTC*, 308) and Henson for Isaac Riley's dissolute character.
- Tom is described as "steady, industrious, pious" (*UTC*, 465), adjectives frequently applied to Henson.
- Tom is described as "an expert and efficient workman in whatever he undertook; and was, both from habit and principle, prompt and faithful" (*UTC*, 500), an apt description of Henson.
- Neither man, in his darkest and most dire circumstances, ever loses his faith in God.

Some of the comparisons are obviously so weak as to be meaningless: that a literary character lives in Kentucky, where Henson was enslaved, is hardly a compelling comparison. Neither is both men being sold to cover debts or being taken down the Mississippi to the slave markets in New Orleans. These events happened to countless enslaved people. It is the number of similarities in the details that lend some credence to the comparison, such as both serving as overseers of the plantation they were enslaved on, both learning to read late in adulthood, both functioning as the religious leaders in their communities, and both finding an axe placed conveniently by the door of the person they have most reason to want to kill.

The most significant similarities between Uncle Tom and Josiah Henson, however, are not in the plot, but in their character—their integrity, intelligence, work ethic, religious fervor, and strength.

The connection between Henson and Uncle Tom was reinforced by the inclusion of *Uncle Tom* in the title of Henson's last two autobiographies and by Stowe's introduction to those works. In the chapter "Mrs. Stowe's Characters," Henson explained that Stowe sent for him and George Clark, his traveling companion, when he was near her home in Andover, Massachusetts, in 1849. Henson related that Stowe asked him to tell her the details about his life. Since he had served as overseer and market man, he was able to speak of his observations of slavery in the region beyond his personal life. Stowe responded, according to Henson, that she hoped his life story "would open the eyes of the people to the enormity of the crime of holding men in bondage."[118]

The problem with Henson's assertion that he met Stowe in Andover in 1849 is that Stowe did not move to Andover until 1852, and by then, she had almost completed the novel. Stowe's son and grandson said that Henson and Stowe met in 1850 in Boston. Henson could, of course, have been mistaken about the year or the place. He was frequently in Massachusetts and well known in abolitionist circles, as was Stowe, so they had many opportunities to meet. Although the time and place cannot be confirmed, it's likely that they met and that his description of their encounter is accurate.

In her brief preface to Henson's autobiography, Stowe refrained from identifying Henson as Uncle Tom. In fact, she opened by stating, "The numerous friends of the author of this work will need no greater recommendation than his name to make it welcome," implying that any possible link between Henson and Uncle Tom is irrelevant. She then mentioned Henson's conversion after hearing his first sermon: "One sermon, one offer of salvation by Christ, was sufficient for him…to make him at once a believer from the heart and a preacher of Jesus." Stowe included only one sentence about Henson that also applies to Uncle Tom: "To the great Christian doctrine of forgiveness of enemies and the returning of good for evil, he was by God's grace made a faithful witness, under circumstances that try men's souls."[119]

THE UNCLE TOM CONUNDRUM

If Henson's connection to Uncle Tom is primarily that he serves as an example of the noble, pious, hardworking enslaved man, why did he include "Uncle Tom" in the title of his memoir and why did Stowe write an introduction to Henson's memoir? Both kept the connection tenuous: Henson's title declares him *an* inspiration, not *the* inspiration for Uncle Tom, and Stowe's preface to his memoir is circumspect about the relationship.

Both Stowe and Henson were famous, accomplished people; both also gained from the connection between their works. Stowe was from a large prominent family. Her father, Lyman Beecher, is widely considered to be the preeminent preacher of his time. Of the eleven siblings, all seven men became preachers, the most effective route to social activism. One brother, Henry Ward Beecher, attained national fame as a preacher and even was asked by President Lincoln to tour Europe speaking on behalf of the Union in the Civil War and to speak at the raising of the United States flag at Fort Sumter after the war. Harriet's sister Catherine founded the Hartford Female Seminary, and her sister Isabella founded the National Woman Suffrage Association. Harriet, who married Calvin Stowe, a theology professor, intended to change the world through writing.

In her introduction to *Uncle Tom's Cabin*, historian Ann Douglas described Stowe as "inheriting no small share of her magnetic father's self-confidence—not to say his self-righteousness—and possessing all of the characteristic Beecher fascination with public interest and the Beecher skill in arousing it."[120] Stowe also famously described her husband as "rich in Greek & Hebrew, Latin & Arabic, & alas! rich in nothing else." Because Stowe unfortunately did not get international rights to *Uncle Tom's Cabin* and because many pirated volumes were published, she did not obtain the riches she deserved. However, promoting a connection with Henson accomplished two goals: it augmented her fame and it underscored her contention that there were many intelligent, talented, venerable men like Uncle Tom and Josiah Henson who deserved both freedom and honor.

Henson's connection to the most famous literary character of the century also had two intertwined advantages. It increased his fame and, consequently, his income. Although Henson generated income through farming his land, the sermons and lectures on education and on slavery that he gave throughout the United States, Canada, and England provided a significant source of income.

Being connected to Uncle Tom increased Henson's appeal as a speaker. He did not, however, confuse himself with the novel's hero. In his post–Civil War speeches, he was frequently introduced as Uncle Tom and typically began with this disclaimer: "It has been spread abroad that 'Uncle Tom is coming,' and that is what has brought you here. Now allow me to say that my name is not Tom, and never was Tom, and that I do not want to have any other name inserted in the newspapers for me than my own. My name is Josiah Henson, always was, and always will be. I never change my colors. I would not if I could, and could not if I would."[121] Despite frequently asserting that he was Josiah Henson, not Uncle Tom, Henson was so widely associated with the fictional Uncle Tom, so often called by that name and so widely believed to be the true Uncle Tom that even his disclaimers didn't alter the public's perception of who he was.

Uncle Tom Redefined

Henson's association with Stowe's Uncle Tom caused his fame to skyrocket. But while the novel was still appearing each week, chapter by chapter, in the *National Era*, stage versions of the play also appeared.

Before the novel was published in book form in March 1852, the first stage version had already been performed in Maryland on January 1852 at the Baltimore Museum. A second version was staged at Alexander Purdy's National Theater in New York in September of the same year. Both productions were short-lived, abbreviated versions. It was the third version that attracted attention: George Aiken created a four-act *Uncle Tom* featuring the then-famous Howard Company actors. The play, which opened on September 27, 1852, at the museum in Troy, New York, ended with the death of Eva. The play was so popular that Aiken added two more acts, concluding the play with Uncle Tom's death.

Jumping Jim Crow. *Wikimedia Commons.*

With the success of the Aiken version, Purdy decided to restage the play, this time with the Howard acting company. The play, which opened on July 1853, had three performances each day. Despite its enhanced theatricality— which eventually included singers, a brass band, and even pyrotechnics—the play remained largely faithful to Stowe's novel. This popular version was staged in major cities.

On November 7, 1853, a new version, written by H.C. Conway, opened at P.T. Barnum's New York theater. Eager to present a version of the play that would not offend any proslavery viewers, Barnum heightened the theatrics and toned down the abolitionist message. This new approach to the story, which reinforced stereotypes and avoided abolitionist rhetoric, set the tone for subsequent productions.

The most popular stage presentations of the era were minstrel shows, which featured white actors in blackface who sang, danced, and performed variety acts, all of which mocked black people. The influence of minstrel shows was clear in all these early stage versions of *Uncle Tom's Cabin*. In January 1854, at New York's Bowery Theater, T.D. Rice, a white actor and playwright famous for his song-and-dance performances in blackface as the clumsy buffoon Jim Crow, played the role of Uncle Tom. His performance mocking Uncle Tom gained popularity, and the transformation from Uncle Tom as a strong, brave, intelligent man into a weak, obsequious fool had begun.

Dramatic versions, known as "Tom Shows," proliferated across the United States and Canada in cities and small towns. In Dresden, Ontario, near the home of Josiah Henson, trains stopped at the station, and a group of performers called Tommers disembarked, performed a Tom Show and then reboarded the same train to travel to the next town.

Hundreds of thousands had read Stowe's *Uncle Tom's Cabin*, but the dramatic productions, minstrel shows, and Tom Shows were so popular that far more people saw a dramatized version than read the novel. Not all depictions of Uncle Tom were negative. In 1903, Edwin S. Porter, working for Thomas Edison, produced the first film of *Uncle Tom's Cabin*, which depicted Uncle Tom as a strong, dignified man of principle who was martyred. And the 1951 Broadway hit of *The King and I*, followed by the 1956 film version, featured a play-within-a-play version, *The Small House of Uncle Thomas*. The stage and film scene, performed by Siamese servants, bears little resemblance to Stowe's novel, pitting the enslaved characters against the evil Legree and ending in their freedom in Canada. Despite these few positive images of Uncle Tom, it was the diminished character of Uncle Tom in minstrel shows that became thoroughly embedded in popular culture. Uncle

Tom was not just the subject of Tom Shows; he appeared in songs, poems, cartoons, and comic books.

Stowe's Uncle Tom was a strong, intelligent, devout, brave defender of the enslaved. But the perception of Uncle Tom had, in a relatively short time, devolved into an old, foolish, shuffling buffoon who was fawning, eager to do whatever a white person requested, and equally willing to betray a black person. It's not surprising that this new Uncle Tom became the worst pejorative a black person could be called by another of his or her race. Originally, to be called "Uncle Tom" was an honor. But by 1919, at the first convention of the Universal Negro Improvement Association in New York City, protesters marched with signs declaring "Uncle Tom's dead and buried." For the protest signs to have had an impact, the name Uncle Tom must have already had a widely accepted derogatory connotation.

Just as Henson had been associated with Uncle Tom in the novel, he became associated with the character in the Tom Shows. The first association increased his reputation and his fame; the second skewed honor into dishonor.

Henson reflected the literary character in his strength, religious fervor, and devotion to all issues affecting black people; however, a few factors lent themselves to the new negative connotation. The custom when greeting people was for a man to show respect by removing his hat, often with a nod or a very slight bow. Since Henson could not lift his arms above his shoulders, he needed to lower his head to his hands to remove his hat. The result appeared to be a low bow, making him look servile.

Both the literary Uncle Tom and Henson had served as overseers, working devotedly to increase their slaveholder's wealth while also protecting the enslaved. In both cases, their exceptional abilities had increased their value, which led to the sale of Uncle Tom and the attempted sale of Henson. However, as time progressed and viewpoints changed, people failed to see the two as extraordinarily intelligent, talented men and instead viewed them as toadies with no personal integrity because of their dedication to serving their slaveholders. This suspicion increased among the residents of Dawn as Henson remained supportive of Scoble in spite of his failure to rebuild the British-American Institute and his contempt for the black population of Dawn.

Changing times altered the perception of Henson in yet another way. In all movements there are rifts, and as Henson had said against his accusers when he was in England, a man dedicated to doing good works will inevitably make enemies. Mary Ann Shadd, the first black woman to found and publish a newspaper, the *Provincial Freeman*, excoriated Henson both for "begging" (i.e., soliciting funds from white philanthropists) and also for the decline of Dawn and the British-American Institute. William P. Newman, pushed out of his position at the institute by Scoble, charged Henson with financial mismanagement and later continued to rail against him through the *Provincial Freeman*. Both Shadd and Newman tarnished the image of Henson and depicted him as a pawn of white men.

Abolitionists disagreed about most issues: the relative value of segregation and integration, whether schools should have trade or academic curricula, and how and where black communities should seek support. One of the most famous rifts was between Booker T. Washington and W.E.B. Du Bois. Washington (1856–1915) was born into slavery, believed in vocational education, and argued that equality would, of necessity, come gradually. A pragmatist, Washington argued that black people needed to become financially independent, which they could best accomplish by creating black-owned businesses in black communities. He urged black people to make the most of their current situation rather than agitating for more, telling them, "Cast down your bucket where you are." To help accomplish this gradual improvement, he established the Tuskegee Institute.

W.E.B. Du Bois (1868–1963) was born free in New England and was raised in a relatively integrated community. He was the first black person to earn a PhD from Harvard. Unlike Washington's call for vocational training, Du Bois urged the creation of a black intelligentsia, which he dubbed the "Talented Tenth." That highly educated group, he argued, would create ways for others to rise.

The differences in the approaches between Washington and Du Bois to moving forward and improving the condition of black people were widely and publicly debated. In 1969, the poet Dudley Randall wrote "Booker T. and W.E.B.," in which the two men expressed their irreconcilable approaches to issues facing black people. The poem concluded, "'It seems to me,' said Booker T.—/ 'I don't agree' / Said W.E.B.'"

Henson was born near the end of the eighteenth century—more than half a century before Washington and Du Bois—so by the time Washington's and Du Bois's philosophies evolved, Henson's major accomplishments were behind him. However, Washington, like Henson, had come out of slavery, and Washington's philosophy reflected Henson's belief in the need for vocational education. Because of the similarity in the two men's contributions to vocational education, their names were sometimes linked. During the twentieth century, Washington was frequently called an Uncle Tom. It's not surprising that Henson, already identified as Stowe's Uncle Tom, would be labeled with the same now negative epithet as Washington.

Josiah Henson was one of the inspirations for Stowe's noble character Uncle Tom; he never in any way resembled the sycophantic character in the Tom plays. It's time to separate the two images, giving Henson credit for embodying the strength, integrity, and courage reflected in Stowe's character and shedding the inaccurate, derogatory conception of Uncle Tom portrayed in popular culture.

Chapter 9

THE LAST YEARS

THE CIVIL WAR

During the Canadian rebellions of 1837–38, black fugitives had been willing to fight to defend their new homeland. When the Civil War broke out in the United States in 1860, many also saw the opportunity to fight in a war that they hoped would defeat slavery. Henson was over sixty, too old to become a soldier, although he said that if he could have carried a gun, he would have gone. Instead, he took it upon himself to talk to others about the war. His message was that "the young and able-bodied ought to go into the field like men, that they should stand up to the rack, and help the government."[122] Henson's eldest son, Tom, who lived in California, enlisted on an armed battleship in San Francisco. Because Henson never again heard from him, he assumed Tom had unfortunately died in the war. His son-in-law, Wheeler, enlisted in Detroit.

The Foreign Enlistment Act of 1819 banned British citizens from serving in a foreign country's military or from recruiting others to do so. During the Civil War, the act carried a penalty of seven years' imprisonment for persuading anyone to enlist. Henson skirted the law by advising people in general terms that they ought to take part in the war, without actually inducing anyone to do so.

In the United States, a bounty system had been established to entice men to enlist by providing cash bonuses. The amount of the bounty varied by state and region. Initially, after the Battle of Fort Sumter, the U.S. Congress enacted a law that provided for bounties up to $300. In some instances, states and local governments added extra amounts, which could total as much as $1,000. The system had two inherent flaws. Bounty jumpers would enlist, collect the bounty, disappear, reenlist somewhere else and collect another bonus. Although bounty jumping was a capital offense, it was not uncommon. A second problem was created by sharpers, conmen who offered to handle enlistees' money for them and then cheated them out of most, if not all, of their bounty.

Henson, 1858. *New York Public Library.*

Although Henson did not try to persuade anyone to enlist, he did offer to help recruits by handling their bounties.

Since the Dawn settlement was only about seventy miles from Detroit, it was relatively easy for fugitives in the area to enlist. Henson told recruits that if they wanted to enlist, he would provide for their families until they could receive the bounty money. Among the first group that went, Henson reported that some lost their bounty money through sharpers. To prevent that problem, he volunteered to accompany the second group.

One man in the second group, John Alexander, came from a poor family, so Henson provided his wife and family with some pork and clothing. Alexander, however, disappeared and claimed that Henson had tried to induce him and some others to enlist, a violation of the Foreign Enlistment Act. When Alexander testified against Henson before a magistrate, Henson's wife sent him a telegraph urging him to stay in Boston because he would be arrested as soon as he returned to Dresden. Henson's initial reaction was to stay away until things calmed down, but then he decided resolutely to return, saying, "I reflected that what I had done was for the cause of Christ, and with good motives; that the war was a righteous war; that the coloured people ought to take some part in it. I said to one of my companions, 'God helping me, I will not run away when I have done no wrong.'"[123]

When Henson returned to Dresden, his family urged him to flee, but he refused. The next morning, William Nellis, the constable who was also Henson's friend, appeared and said to him, "Mr. Henson, you are my

Henson House, Dresden. *Uncle Tom's Cabin Historic Site.*

prisoner in the name of the Queen. Here is a writ for you."[124] After eating a leisurely breakfast, Henson said to Nellis that he was ready but pointed out that the writ specified that Nellis had to *take* him. Henson denied Nellis the rent of his horse and wagon and suggested that since he would not walk with Nellis, he could perhaps be transported in a wheelbarrow. Henson gave his word that Nellis could leave and that he would appear before the magistrate shortly.

When Henson appeared, he discovered that he was not allowed to plead his case or have a lawyer speak for him. Two magistrates were assigned to the case. One resented Henson because of his interference in a prior suit against the trustees of the British-American Institute. The other, Squire Terrace, was Henson's friend. Since the two could not agree, the case was forwarded to a third magistrate. This next official, hearing the two sides, also could not reach a conclusion, so the case was taken to Mr. McLean, the county attorney, another of Henson's friends. McLean, knowing Henson's character and knowledge of the law, doubted that Henson would have induced anyone to enlist. McLean suspected something was awry but said that if Alexander's accusations were true, nothing would spare Henson the seven-year prison sentence. He then asked Henson for his version of the events. Henson explained that he had sent provisions to Alexander's family,

Henson House interior. *Uncle Tom's Cabin Historic Site.*

which he would do for anyone in need, but it was not intended as bribery to get him to enlist.

McLean said, "We all know Mr. Henson's character, that he is an honest, upright, Christian man. Now what is the character of his accuser?" It was Saturday, so McLean postponed his verdict until Monday to have an opportunity to learn more about Alexander. As in other crises he had faced, Henson put his trust in God, saying, "How I should get released from the legal net that was spread over me I did not know, but I trusted in God; I knew he had delivered me many, many times before from the lions' den, and, like Daniel of olden times, I now put my faith in him."[125]

Henson was allowed to return home for the weekend on Saturday afternoon. That evening, a man appeared at Henson's home and said that he had encountered a Mr. Smith at the river. Smith, who was loading a boat prior to departing, said he lived in the same district as Alexander. Smith claimed that Alexander was known to be a thief and that after a writ for his arrest had been taken out, he had fled. He also added that Alexander had falsely accused a man of enticing others to enlist. Henson received permission from the constable to visit his friend Squire Terrace to pass on the information.

Early on Monday morning, Terrace went to the riverbank and hailed Smith's boat, which had just set sail. After the boat returned to shore,

Terrace spoke with Smith, who said he had worked with Alexander and called him "a mean, lying thief." Terrace subpoenaed Smith to appear in court at nine o'clock in the morning. Both parties, Alexander and Henson, appeared in court that morning before Squire McDonald. Because Alexander had not anticipated that a witness would appear to support Henson, he was confident that he would win the case. Smith testified that Alexander was "one of the greatest rogues out of prison" and added that Alexander would be in prison had he not jumped bail. The case was immediately decided in Henson's favor.

Shortly after the case was resolved, Henson became embroiled in the law a second time. Alexander Pool, a friend of his who lived nearby, said that his son and his brother-in-law intended to enlist. Pool wanted Henson to take the men to Detroit to ensure that they got their bounty. Henson was clear that he did not intend to become involved in another trial and would not encourage them to enlist. Still, he recognized that Pool should receive some bounty money to help him with expenses. After repeated urgings from Pool, Henson agreed to take the two men to Detroit. When the two registered as brothers, Martin and Basil Pool, Henson was suspicious that they might become bounty jumpers, but both men enlisted and fought in several battles. The bounty for the two totaled $1,200. Henson, as their representative, sent $100 to the two enlistees and returned $1,100 to Alexander Pool, who gave him $400 for his expenses. Pool had never possessed so much money, and Henson reported that "he squandered it in dissipation."

When the two soldiers returned from war, Alexander Pool claimed that he had never received the money from Henson. They contacted a lawyer, who referred them to Squire McDonald, so Henson was once again in front of the man who had settled the previous case. McDonald suggested that instead of filing a suit, they go to Henson and see if he would repay the amount over time. Henson repeated that he had not kept the bounty money and asked to see Basil Davis's discharge papers. The papers revealed that he had enlisted under the false name of Basil Pool and that he had been "discharged under false pretenses." Clearly, Henson's original suspicion that he would be a bounty jumper had been correct. This issue went no further. However, Henson had finally learned that he "had better let volunteers gain wisdom and experience for themselves, without giving them either advice or personal assistance."[126]

The Third Trip to England

Throughout the years, Henson had continued to preach. As a Methodist Episcopal Elder, he said he traveled over a three-hundred-mile territory in Canada preaching, establishing new churches, holding meetings, and attending conferences. He had, he said, remained interested in all efforts involving the emancipation and the progress of black people.

Reverend Thomas Hughes, secretary of the Colonial and Continental Missionary Church Society in Canada, was a longtime friend of Henson's. Hughes, born in England, moved to Canada in 1856 to work for the Mission to Fugitive Slaves in Canada. When the Colonial Church and School Society opened a mission in Dresden, Hughes moved there with his family and became an Anglican priest in 1859. He founded a school and two churches in Dresden and established close ties to the fugitive communities in the area. It was Hughes who recommended to Henson that he try to recoup the money he had lost in the seven-year lawsuit with Scoble by returning to London to preach and speak. In his letter of recommendation, Hughes explained Henson's financial need, saying that Henson had borne the entire cost of the suit, and when the case was settled, it was determined that the trustees had no power to reimburse Henson out of the estate.

Armed with the letter by Hughes and with several other letters, all testifying to both his astounding life story and to his integrity and good character, Henson set off for England again, this time at age eighty-seven. It had been twenty-five years since his previous visit. Two London friends, Samuel Morley and George Sturge, set up a fund for Henson and each donated fifty pounds sterling to it. In addition to contributions from other friends and acquaintances, Henson received many donations from Quakers, who had aided him in his escape and in endeavors throughout his life.

In England, Henson met Professor Fowler, a phrenologist who created a lengthy description of Henson's character by examining his skull. Although phrenology was largely discredited by scientists in England by this time, it was still popular. When John Lobb, the managing editor of the weekly publication the *Christian Age*, published the account of Fowler's description of Henson, the demand was so great that he had to reissue the paper twice. Since Lobb was acquainted with many evangelical London ministers, he made the arrangements for Henson's many public appearances in London. He also became the editor of the last two iterations of Henson's autobiography.

On March 5, 1877, Henson, accompanied by his second wife, Nancy, and John Lobb, traveled to Windsor Castle to meet Queen Victoria. After being

Henson with Queen Victoria. *Uncle Tom's Cabin Historic Site.*

served a luncheon, they were presented to Queen Victoria, Prince Leopold and Princess Beatrice. Queen Victoria expressed surprise and delight at "the clergyman's hale and hearty looks, considering his great age."[127] When complimented on his looks by the queen, Henson purportedly replied, "That's what all the ladies tell me." Queen Victoria had first seen Henson at the 1851 World's Fair and was familiar with both his amazing life story and his association with Uncle Tom. The photograph of herself that she presented to Henson, signed "Victoria Reg., 1877," became one of his most prized possessions.

On behalf of the fugitives in Canada, Henson thanked the queen for her protection. Prior to emancipation, Queen Victoria had been a beacon of hope for the enslaved hoping to escape to Canada. She proclaimed in the 1840s that every enslaved person from the United States who reached Canada would be under the protection of the laws of the British Empire. Victoria's name was well known to escapees through the song "I'm on My Way to Canada," which was sung to the tune of "Oh, Susanna":

> *Oh, I heard Queen Victoria say,*
> *That if we would forsake*
> *Our native land of slavery,*

And come across the lake;
That she was standing on the shore,
With arms extended wide,
To give us all a peaceful home
Beyond the rolling tide
Farewell, old master, don't think hard of me,
I'm on my way to Canada, where all the slaves are free.

Queen Victoria had given permission for everyone at Windsor Castle to meet Henson—whom she referred to as Uncle Tom—so the Hensons and Lobb were escorted throughout the castle. After the visit with the queen, Henson, still accompanied by Lobb, went to Scotland and continued his speaking engagements. By the time they sailed for home in April 1877, Henson had earned enough money to pay off all his mortgages and live comfortably.

Return to Maryland

In December of the same year, Henson's wife, Nancy, wanted to visit Baltimore, Maryland, where she had once lived and where her sister still lived. Henson also wanted to return to the Isaac Riley plantation in Montgomery County, Maryland, where he had spent so many formative years. The Hensons set out on Christmas Eve and arrived in Baltimore on December 26. They stayed in Baltimore until early March and then headed to Washington, D.C.

As overseer on Isaac Riley's plantation, Henson had frequently gone to Washington to sell the farm's produce. This time, his destination in Washington was the White House. On March 4, 1877, Rutherford B. Hayes was inaugurated as the nineteenth president of the United States. In under two weeks, Hayes nominated Frederick Douglass as U.S. marshal of the District of Columbia. On behalf of Henson, Douglass sent a letter to President Hayes asking that Henson be invited to the White House. Henson's description of his visit is brief: "I called on his Excellency President Hayes, in his office, while Mrs. Hayes very kindly showed my wife through the house. The President was pleased to be very gracious, and when I rose to take leave, after a pleasant little chat about my trip across the water, he gave me a very cordial invitation to call again, should I ever pay another visit to the capital."[128]

Henson portrait. *Uncle Tom's Cabin Historic Site.*

Within about one year, Henson had met the queen of England and the president of the United States. His next visit—the old Isaac Riley plantation—was in stark contrast. It had been almost a half century since Henson had been enslaved to Isaac Riley. He assumed the plantation would be much as it had been when he had last seen it. He described the plantation as he imagined it: "I still pictured to myself the great fertile plantation, with its throngs of busy labourers sowing the seed, tilling the ground, and reaping the valuable harvests as of yore. I saw the 'great house,' well furnished and sheltering a happy, luxurious, and idle family....I saw the barns and storehouses bursting with plenty." Instead, he found "the most desolate, demoralized place one can imagine."[129] The fields were overgrown with brush and weeds, the fences had disappeared, the trees in the orchards were dead and the house was dilapidated.

Matilda Riley, long widowed, was frail and in ill health. At first, she didn't recognize Henson, but then she recalled their overseer from years ago, Si Henson, and to assure herself it was really him, she felt his crippled arms. Recognizing him, she exclaimed, "Why, Si, you are a gentleman!" to which he responded, "I always was, madam."[130] When she complained of her dire poverty, Henson asked her why she hadn't kept some of her enslaved workers. She explained that she couldn't—some had died, some had been sold, and Lincoln freed the rest. When Henson asked why she hadn't kept some of the workers by paying them, she responded in surprise, saying that they weren't worth paying.

Before he left the plantation, Henson visited his mother's grave. He had never forgotten the spiritual guidance she had given him as a boy. He prayed that he would always live in a manner that honored her and that when his death came, he would "fall asleep in the Lord" as did his mother.

Chapter 10

HENSON'S LEGACY

HENSON'S DEATH

After returning to Canada from Maryland, Henson lived a relatively quiet life, although he continued to speak and preach. Of the four sons he and Charlotte brought to Canada in 1830, Tom, the eldest, had presumably died in the Civil War. Henson described his second-oldest son, Isaac, as "clever and godly." Isaac was educated in London, England, through the generosity of Henson's English friends, became a Wesleyan Methodist minister, and died at age thirty-seven. His third son and namesake, Josiah, helped Henson on the farm, although he wanted to become a shoemaker. After he married, young Josiah and his wife moved to Jackson, Michigan, where he apprenticed himself to an English boot and shoe maker while his wife worked as a laundress. After his apprenticeship, Henson said, young Josiah was deemed as good a shoemaker as the man who had taught him the trade. Peter, the fourth son, stayed with Henson and farmed the land. Henson said that all four of his surviving daughters—whom he doesn't name—married and could read and write well. One was even educated at Oberlin College at Oberlin, Ohio, for two years. With the death of Tom and Isaac, only two of the four sons he and Charlotte had brought to Canada were alive, and Peter, Josiah and his four daughters were all that remained of the twelve children born to him.

Henson was in his early nineties when he preached his last sermon in Hamilton, Ontario. It was a long, rambling address in which he claimed to be the true Uncle Tom—a title he had always denied. This once fiercely intelligent and honest man may well have been suffering from dementia at the end of his life.

On May 5, 1883, he died at his home in Dresden after a three-day illness. His obituary appeared in newspapers across Canada, the United States, and England. The obituary in the *London Times* on May 23, 1883, listed his cause of death as paralysis, "aggravated by the cruel treatment he received in slavery."[131] Henson's funeral was elaborate. Bishop Walter R. Hawkins, who had once been enslaved with Henson on Amos Riley's plantation and was now the head of the British Methodist Episcopal Church in Canada, conducted the funeral. Nine preachers spoke and prayed, and both the church and churchyard were filled with mourners. A brass band preceded his hearse, which was followed to the cemetery by fifty wagons.

Despite his fame, Henson had never become a wealthy man, although he certainly lived a comfortable life. In his will, he provided for his wife, children, and grandchildren. To his wife, Nancy, he left all the "household furniture and effects—one cow, one of the black mares and the buggy and harness and the annual payment hereinafter mentioned." His son Peter received his gold watch and chain and half of the proceeds from the sale of a Hambletonian thoroughbred stallion. His daughter Julia Wheeler inherited about two and a half acres. In addition to his provisions for his other children and grandchildren, he also bequeathed $100 to the British Episcopal Methodist Church in Dresden.[132]

After Henson's death, Nancy sold the house in Canada and moved to Michigan. The uninhabited house, which was located on William Chapple's farm, became a tourist attraction. Chapple promoted the site with his book, *The Story of Uncle Tom*, published by Uncle Tom's Cabin and Museum. Some people wanted to see the house where Father Henson, the spiritual leader of their community, had lived. Others wanted to see the house where the Uncle Tom who inspired the famous novel had lived. Chapple's solution was simple: he placed a pot outside the door for tourists to drop in contributions for admission.

For decades after Henson's death, the house and grave site were largely untended. However, Henson had joined the Black Masons during a trip to Boston and, upon his return to Canada, had joined Dresden's Mount Moriah Lodge No. 4. Throughout the 1920s, black Masonic organizations made pilgrimages to his grave.

In 1930, the Independent Order of the Daughters of the Empire (IODE), a Canadian women's organization, began to care for the previously untended

Henson's memorial gravestone. *Photo by Edna M. Troiano.*

grave site, and the following year, the Dresden & District Horticultural Society agreed to assist the IODE chapter in maintaining the site. In 1933, the horticultural society asked the Camden Council for permission to take over the plot, and in May of that year, it received permission to tend and beautify the Henson family cemetery.

Mr. Jack Thomson became the owner of the Henson house after William Chapple. Thomson twice moved the house, reorienting its position. He also built and opened a museum on the site in 1964. Twenty years later, he sold the museum to the County of Kent.

In 1995, the house became the property of the St. Clair Parkway Commission. The commission undertook a $1.2 million restoration, which included strengthening inner beams, replacing clapboard, replicating the original porch based on an early photo, replacing the cedar shingle roof, and removing the fireplace, which was not original to the building. In 2005, one year before the St. Clair Parkway Commission was disbanded, the commission transferred ownership of the museum to the Ontario Heritage Trust, which still maintains ownership. The Henson family cemetery and the British-American Institute cemetery, although maintained by the Ontario Heritage Trust, are the property of the Municipality of Chatham-Kent.

UNCLE TOM'S CABIN HISTORIC SITE

Today, the Uncle Tom's Cabin Historic Site, which consists of an interpretive center and an outdoor museum, is situated on five acres of land that once housed the British-American Institute. The site is run by two descendants of the original settlers of the Dawn community: site manager Steven Cook and program assistant Brenda Lambkin.

The interpretive center includes a theater, a gallery, and a gift shop. Visitors are introduced to Henson by a video shown in the North Star Theater. The Underground Railroad Freedom Gallery highlights events in Henson's life and features nineteenth-century artifacts, including an early edition of his first autobiography, *The Life of Josiah Henson, Formerly a Slave, Now an Inhabitant of Canada, as Narrated by Himself*. The display in the gallery provides context for Henson's life through a historical overview of the lives of the enslaved, from being captured in Africa and sold in the United States to finding freedom in Canada. For non-English-speaking visitors, pamphlets are available in German, French, Dutch and Japanese.

The worldwide popularity and impact of Stowe's *Uncle Tom's Cabin* is demonstrated through a display of copies of the novel in twenty-four languages; in addition to the many European editions, there are editions

Steven Cook. *Uncle Tom's Cabin Historic Site.*

Uncle Tom's Cabin Historic Site Interpretive Center. *Uncle Tom's Cabin Historic Site.*

from countries around the globe, including Turkey, India, Korea, Japan, Lebanon, and Israel.

The gallery provides so much information that one visit may not be enough for most tourists. However, the historic gems lie outside. As visitors step through the rear door of the interpretive center, they enter an outdoor museum taking them back into the world of the Dawn settlement. They can explore Henson's house, the Henson family cemetery, the Pioneer Church, the Harris house, the sawmill, the smokehouse, and the British-American Institute cemetery.

Visitors can enter the Henson house, built circa 1850, where Josiah and Nancy were living when Henson died in 1883. Although the house has been moved, it has always remained on lands that were once part of the British-American Institute. In 1993–94, the house was under restoration to bring it back to circa 1850. Entering the house, visitors can picture what daily life was like in Dawn for Josiah and his wife, Nancy. Henson was living a comfortable life, one he could not have imagined when as a boy he slept on the crowded dirt floor of Isaac Riley's slave quarters.

The Pioneer Church is next to the Henson house. The church, although not the one where Henson preached in the Dawn settlement, is typical of rural churches of the time. Built in 1850, it was moved to the site in 1964 and contains the original organ from the church where Henson once preached. Inside the entrance is a sign with the lyrics of Henson's favorite hymn, "The Rest of Heaven": "There is a land of pure delight where saints immortal reign. Infinite day excludes the night and pleasures banish pain."

Henson's grave is located near the church in the Henson family cemetery. The memorial monument "where his abused and honoured bones lie" is marked with the Masonic symbol and topped by a crown signifying his visit with Queen Victoria. Next to the monument is a plaque erected in 1999 by the Historic Sites and Monuments Board of Canada summarizing Henson's life and achievements. On the worn surface, the stone carver's error is still visible: the monument states that Henson died in July, two months later than his actual death. The family cemetery seems small, with only twenty-one headstones, most too worn to be read; however, more than three hundred people are buried there. Across the road from the Henson family cemetery is

British-American Institute cemetery. *Photo by Edna M. Troiano.*

Smokehouse. *Photo by Edna M. Troiano.*

the British-American Institute cemetery, the burial place for members of the Dawn settlement and the British-American Institute.

An original smokehouse from the area has been preserved—the roofed, hollowed-out trunk of a sycamore tree used to cure and preserve meat. Just feet away from the smokehouse is a reconstructed sawmill, identical to the one used to produce lumber from trees cleared from the land. Next to the sawmill stands a black walnut tree, a reminder of the once plentiful trees used to make the polished boards Henson exhibited at the London World's Fair and sold in the United States and Canada to generate revenue for the British-American Institute.

A second house on the site, the Harris house, is representative of the homes of many of the area's black settlers. Built circa 1890, the house is one of the oldest structures left in the area. The two-story house, which has a post-and-beam frame with clapboard siding, was moved to the Uncle Tom's Cabin Historic Site from Dresden in the 1960s.

A stream of sightseers passes through the museum each day. Some visitors are astonished to learn that the character of Uncle Tom was inspired by a real person; others are impressed that descendants of the original nineteenth-century Dawn settlers maintain the site where their ancestors settled in Canada. Each year, about four thousand students travel to the museum. The school groups are introduced to Henson, sometimes for the first time. The presentation for students, both fact-filled and fun, includes a scavenger hunt. In addition to the nearly eight thousand visitors who tour the Uncle Tom's Cabin Historic Site each year, the museum staff gives presentations at churches and schools, making Josiah Henson still a presence in the community to which he devoted so much of his life.

The Uncle Tom's Cabin Historic Site has remained Dresden's main tourist attraction. Like Henson, many of the enslaved who fled the United States found a safe place in the area where they could build homes, get an education, and earn a living. Dresden served as an important terminus on the Underground Railroad, but the Dresden area was no Eden: as the black population increased, so did racism. In the 1940s, racial discrimination was still rampant. In its article "Jim Crow Lives in Dresden," *Macleans* magazine cited Dresden as one of Canada's most bitterly racially divided cities. Black people, for example, could not eat in any of the three restaurants or, more significantly, get a job in any field other than manual labor.[133] Ironically, Dresden existed both as a welcoming site for refugees and a center of Jim Crow activities.

HENSON'S HERITAGE

On September 16, 1983, Henson was honored with a commemorative stamp marking the 100th anniversary of his death. Because of his importance as a spiritual and community leader, he became the first black person to be portrayed on a Canadian stamp. In 1999, the Historic Sites and Monuments Board of Canada named him a National Historic Person. Ten years later, in 2009, the U-Haul Companies of Eastern and Western Ontario came to the Uncle Tom's Cabin Historic Site to showcase one of its new trucks, part of a fleet of 1,700 commemorating the Underground Railroad in Ontario. The graphic along the side of the trucks depicts the Henson house, Harriet Tubman, and a map of the province marked with Underground Railroad routes.

Henson lives on not only at the sites that memorialize him or in stamps, plaques, and moving vans but also in his descendants. Barbara Carter, Henson's great-great-granddaughter, is a descendant of Henson's son

Left: Henson portrait. *Uncle Tom's Cabin Historic Site*.

Below: Barbara Carter at U-Haul unveiling. *Uncle Tom's Cabin Historic Site*.

Peter. Although aware of Henson, Carter said that she wasn't particularly interested in her family's connection to him as she was growing up. However, the more she learned about Henson, the more her interest in him increased. Thomson, the original owner of the museum, invited Carter to public events and encouraged her interest in her famous ancestor. As an adult, she worked in the museum from the 1970s to the 1990s, and in 1993, Carter greeted one of the site's famous visitors, Rosa Parks.

In her work as museum curator, Carter realized that the thread of Henson's narrative had become lost in the museum's collections, so she helped refocus the museum's artifacts to incorporate the history of slavery, the Underground Railroad, the life of black people in the area, and the life of Henson. She recommended that an advisory committee be created to get feedback from the community. The St. Clair Parkway Commission established the committee, and Carter integrated the advisory committee's feedback in the design and the contents of both the 1995 Josiah Henson Interpretive Center and the open-air buildings and structures behind the center.

Carter's interest in Henson extended beyond his life in Dresden. In 1993, she and her daughter, Kathy, took a bus tour of Henson sites. They toured the Josiah Henson house in Montgomery County, Maryland, and while in Owensboro, Kentucky, they saw a production of *Josiah!*, a musical drama based on Henson's life.

When asked if she felt any personal connection to her famous ancestor, Carter replied that she did not. However, Brenda Lambkin immediately chimed in saying that Carter's life centered on her unshakeable faith, as did Henson's. Carter countered that faith was of necessity central to the lives of many black people. Steven Cook added another correlation he had noticed. Like Henson, he said, when Carter had a goal in mind, she "had a way of making things happen."

Two generations further removed from Carter, Mia Lewis is Henson's great-great-great-great-granddaughter, the descendant of Henson's daughter Elizabeth. Lewis's family is from Michigan, but she currently lives in Charlotte, North Carolina. Lewis cannot recall when she learned she was descended from Henson because she was very young; from her vantage point, she had always known of her connection to Henson and thought of him as a unifying force in her far-flung, extended family. Every family home, Lewis said, contains photos of Henson and copies of his books, and the connection to Henson remains a source of pride.

When she was growing up, Lewis learned that the family believed Henson was an inspiration for Stowe's character, based partly on Stowe's

Mia Lewis. *Photo by Tyrone Anderson.*

own comments and partly on Uncle Tom's traits: his deep, unshakeable faith, honesty, integrity, dedication to saving others, intelligence, and skill. Lewis was surprised, and then confused, when she first heard other children at school refer to Uncle Tom with scorn. For a while, she didn't want to admit that she was descended from him. But as she grew, she understood how Henson's reputation had been skewed from that of a man of faith, accomplishments, and integrity into the butt of minstrel shows, a character that in no way resembled Josiah Henson.

As an adult, Lewis retains a deep connection to the Henson descendants and attends family reunions. Like Carter, she has traveled to Montgomery County, Maryland, to tour the Riley/Bolton House at the Josiah Henson Special Park, and in 2016, she went to La Plata, Maryland, to see Henson's birthplace at La Grange.

Lewis credited her family's awareness and admiration of Henson to her great-uncle, Walter Irving Dean, the family historian and great-great-grandson of Henson. Dean, Lewis noted, was "instrumental in making sure our family was very aware of who Henson was, our relation to him, and his wonderful works and contributions."

After Dean's death in 2003, Michelle Dunham Roberts continued to foster connections among Henson's many descendants by building the Henson Nevels Family website (http://hensonnevelsfamily.com), which aims to connect descendants all over the world. Even though Josiah Henson's descendants are scattered across the globe, his spirit lives on in them and in the places in the United States and Canada that keep his remarkable story alive.

CHRONOLOGY OF HENSON'S LIFE

Three dates have been posited as the year of Henson's birth: 1789, 1796, and 1798. Current research at La Grange in Charles County, Maryland, supports the latest of the three dates. Events marked "circa" are estimates based on a 1798 birthdate.

1798	Henson is born enslaved at La Grange in Charles County, Maryland.
1805	Henson is sold at auction to Adam Robb and then bartered to Isaac Riley.
circa 1810	Henson is severely beaten for attempting to learn to read.
circa 1816	At age eighteen, Henson is converted to Christianity.
circa 1818	Henson is beaten and maimed.
circa 1820	Henson, at age twenty-two, marries Charlotte, enslaved on a nearby plantation.
1825	Henson leads Isaac Riley's enslaved to Amos Riley's Kentucky plantation.
1825–28	Henson serves as overseer on Amos Riley's plantation.
1828–29	Henson returns from Amos Riley's Kentucky plantation to Isaac Riley's Maryland plantation. Isaac Riley presents Henson with manumission papers.
1830	Henson is taken to New Orleans to be sold but is able to return to Kentucky to escort Amos Riley Jr., who was ill. Henson, Charlotte, and their four children escape to Canada.

1834	Henson explores the land on foot, looking for an area suitable for a self-sufficient black community, and decides that the Dawn would be ideal.
1836	With others, Henson moves to Colchester to farm the land rented by McCormick.
1838	Henson and Hiram Wilson call a convention in London, Ontario, to discuss the use of funds supplied by James C. Fuller.
1842	Henson and his family move to Dawn. The British-American Institute is opened.
1849	Henson publishes his first autobiography, *The Life of Josiah Henson, Formerly a Slave, Now an Inhabitant of Canada*.
1850	Isaac Riley dies. Henson is elected president of the newly formed Fugitive Union Society.
1851	Henson exhibits black walnut milled at Dawn at the London World's Fair.
1852	Henson's wife Charlotte dies. The British-American Institute is closed. Harriet Beecher Stowe publishes *Uncle Tom's Cabin*.
circa 1856	Henson marries Nancy Gamble.
1858	Henson frees his brother, John. Henson publishes his second autobiography, *Truth Stranger than Fiction: Father Henson's Story of His Own Life*.
1876	Henson publishes his third autobiography, *Uncle Tom's Story of His Life: An Autobiography of the Rev. Josiah Henson (Mrs. Harriet Beecher Stowe's "Uncle Tom")*.
1877	Henson meets Queen Victoria and is presented with a portrait of her. Henson meets President Rutherford B. Hayes at the White House.
1881	Henson publishes his fourth autobiography, *Autobiography of Josiah Henson, an Inspiration for Harriet Beecher Stowe's Uncle Tom*.
1883	Henson dies in Dresden on May 5.

NOTES

Chapter 1

1. Webster et al., *In Search of Josiah Henson's Birthplace*, 103–4.
2. Henson was never more than semiliterate; however, he narrated four autobiographies: *The Life of Josiah Henson, Formerly a Slave, Now an Inhabitant of Canada, as Narrated by Himself* (1849); *Truth Stranger than Fiction: Father Henson's Story of His Own Life* (1858); *Uncle Tom's Story of His Life: An Autobiography of the Rev. Josiah Henson(Mrs. Harriet Beecher Stowe's "Uncle Tom")* (1876); and *An Autobiography of Josiah Henson: An Inspiration for Harriet Beecher Stowe's Uncle Tom* (1881). The first version was dictated to Samuel A. Eliot. The third and fourth were edited by John Lobb. There is no consensus about the second version. All quotations and references are from the 1881 autobiography, which is the last and most complete.
3. Lee, *Price of Nationhood*, 239–43.
4. Webster et al., *In Search of Josiah Henson's Birthplace*, 19.
5. Henson, *Autobiography of Josiah Henson*, 16.
6. Ibid.
7. Ibid., 17.
8. Klapthor and Brown, *History of Charles County Maryland*, 119.
9. The crew from St. Mary's College of Maryland, under the direction of Dr. King, consisted of Assistant Project Archaeologist Rebecca Webster; Assistant Archaeologists Morgan Jenkins-Houk, Kyle Moore, Lydia Roca and Max Sickler, who worked both in the lab and the field; Lab Technician

Demilade Adebayo; Social Media Coordinator Cody Dorsey; and Project Archaeologist Scott M. Strickland. Charles County High School interns Jakob Gammons and Chadeya Miller worked at the site June 20–24 and June 27.

10. Heim, "In Search of 'Uncle Tom,'" *Washington Post*, B2.
11. Lee, *Price of Nationhood*, 330–31.
12. Webster et al., *In Search of Josiah Henson's Birthplace*, 35.
13. Heim, "In Search of 'Uncle Tom,'" *Washington Post*, B2.
14. Henson, *Autobiography of Josiah Henson*, 14.
15. Ibid., 15.
16. Webster et al., *In Search of Josiah Henson's Birthplace*, 1.

Chapter 2

17. Henson, *Autobiography of Josiah Henson*, 18.
18. Ibid.
19. Bleby, *Josiah*, 25.
20. Henson, *Autobiography of Josiah Henson*, 19.
21. Douglass, *Narrative of the Life of Frederick Douglass*, 21.
22. Henson, *Autobiography of Josiah Henson*, 21.
23. Douglass, *Narrative of the Life of Frederick Douglass*, 16.
24. Henson, *Autobiography of Josiah Henson*, 19–20.
25. Douglass, *Narrative of the Life of Frederick Douglass*, 16.
26. Henson, *Autobiography of Josiah Henson*, 20.
27. Ibid., 22.
28. Ibid.
29. Ibid., 138.
30. Ibid., 135.
31. Ibid., 24.
32. Ibid., 27.
33. Ibid., 28.
34. Ibid., 29.
35. Ibid., 31.
36. John Miller Associates, "Executive Summary, *Historical Structure Report for the Riley House/Josiah Henson Site*, iii.

Chapter 3

37. Henson, *Autobiography of Josiah Henson*, 33.
38. Ibid., 34.
39. Ibid., 35.
40. Ibid., 35–36.
41. Ibid., 36.
42. Ibid.
43. Ibid., 37.
44. Ibid., 40.
45. Ibid., 42.
46. Ibid., 46.
47. Ibid., 47.
48. Ibid., 48.
49. Ibid., 139.
50. Stowe, *Uncle Tom's Cabin or, Life Among the Lowly*, 365.
51. Henson, *Autobiography of Josiah Henson*, 50–51.
52. Ibid., 51.
53. Ibid., 53.
54. Ibid., 55.
55. Ibid., 56.
56. Ibid., 57.
57. Ibid., 58.
58. "Si Henson, the Original of Mrs. Stowe's Great Novel," *Owensboro Messenger & Examiner*, 1.
59. Hager, "Uncle Tom Lived in Daviess," *Messenger Inquirer*, 25.
60. Shulins, "Area Man Leads Fight to Recognize 'Uncle Tom' Link," *The Gleaner*, 3.
61. Froehlich, "Proclamation of Recognition," Kentucky Room, Daviess County Library.
62. Coady, "Daviess Countians Claim 'Uncle Tom' as One of Their Own," *Courier-Journal*, 1.
63. Lawrence, "Memory of Henson's Life Is Fading in Daviess County," *Messenger Inquirer*, 1.
64. *Auction Central News*, "Plantation Papers to Go on Display in Kentucky."

Chapter 4

65. *Underground Railroad*, Official National Park Handbook, 2.
66. Douglass, *Narrative of the Life of Frederick Douglass*, 81.
67. Ibid., 198–201.
68. Brent, *Incidents in the Live of a Slave Girl*, 473.
69. Henson, *Autobiography of Josiah Henson*, 59.
70. Ibid., 60.
71. Ibid., 61.
72. Ibid., 63.
73. Ibid., 64.
74. Ibid.
75. Ibid., 65.
76. Ibid., 69.
77. Ibid.

Chapter 5

78. Ibid., 72–73.
79. Ibid., 75.
80. Ibid., 77.
81. Carter and Carter, *Stepping Back in Time*, 13–17.
82. Henson, *Autobiography of Josiah Henson*, 128.
83. Ibid., 79.
84. Ibid., 87.
85. Craig, "Kentucky Slave Inspired Stowe Novel," *Courier-Journal*, 15.
86. Henson, *Autobiography of Josiah Henson*, 91.
87. Ibid., 126.
88. Ibid., 95.
89. Longfellow, *The Life of Henry Wadsworth Longfellow*, 48.
90. Wilson, "Letter to Brother Whipple," October 1, 1850.
91. Buxton Museum National Historic Site and Museum.

Chapter 6

92. Henson, *Autobiography of Josiah Henson*, 97.
93. *The Liberator*, "Josiah Henson—Caution," 4.

94. Henson, *Autobiography of Josiah Henson*, 97.
95. Ibid., 98.
96. Ibid., 101.
97. Ibid., 105.

Chapter 7

98. Ibid., 107–8.
99. Ibid., 142.
100. Ibid.
101. Ibid., 120.
102. *The Liberator*, "John Scoble," 2.
103. Henson, *Autobiography of Josiah Henson*, 121.
104. Ibid.
105. Ibid., 122.
106. Ibid., 123.
107. Ibid., 123–124.
108. Colored Conventions, "Bringing Nineteenth-Century Black Organization to Digital Life," 101–4.

Chapter 8

109. Stowe, *Key to Uncle Tom's Cabin*, 5.
110. Ibid., 30.
111. Ibid., 23.
112. Ibid., 26.
113. Henson, *Autobiography of Josiah Henson*, 116.
114. Ibid., 117.
115. Ibid., 113–14.
116. Ibid., 117.
117. Stowe, "The Original Uncle Tom," *Evening News*, 2.
118. Henson, *Autobiography of Josiah Henson*, 113.
119. Ibid., 3.
120. Douglass, "Introduction," *Uncle Tom's Cabin*, 10.
121. Winks, "Introduction," *An Autobiography of Josiah Henson*, xxii.

Chapter 9

122. Henson, *Autobiography of Josiah Henson*, 128.
123. Ibid., 129.
124. Ibid.
125. Ibid., 131.
126. Ibid., 134.
127. Ibid., 151.
128. Ibid., 158.
129. Ibid., 158–59.
130. Ibid., 160.

Chapter 10

131. *London Times*, "Obituary," 10.
132. Henson Nevels Family, "Will and Testament of Josiah Henson."
133. Katz, "Jim Crow Lives in Dresden," *Macleans*, 8–9.

BIBLIOGRAPHY

Abdul-Alim, Jamaal. "Uncle Tom Uncovered." *Diverse Issues in Higher Education* 33, no. 18 (2016). https://www.questia.com/magazine/1P3-4207695881/uncle-tom-uncovered.

African-American Registry. http://www.aaregistry.org.

Anfenson-Comeau, Jamie. "Archaeological Dig Finds Signs of Abolitionist's Birthplace." *Maryland Independent,* June 16, 2016, A3.

Auction Central News. "Plantation Papers to Go on Display in Kentucky." www.liveauctioneers.com.

Beattie, Jessie L. *Black Moses: The Real Uncle Tom.* Toronto: Ryerson Press, 1957.

Bleby, Henry. *Josiah: The Maimed Fugitive.* London: Wesleyan Conference Office, 1873. Reprint, 2010, CreateSpace.

Brent, Linda. *Incidents in the Live of a Slave Girl.* Boston: published for the author, 1861. Reprinted in *The Classic Slave Narratives.* Edited by Henry Louis Gates Jr. New York: Signet Classics, 2002.

Buxton Museum National Historic Site and Museum. "Virtual Education." http://www.buxtonmuseum.com/history/virtual-education.

Canada's Human Rights History. "Dresden and Racial Discrimination." http://historyofrights.ca/encyclopaedia/main-events/dresden-racial-discrimination.

Carter, Marie, and Jeffrey Carter. *Stepping Back in Time: Along the Trillium Trail in Dresden.* Dresden, Ontario: Catherine McVean Chapter, Independent Order of the Daughters of the Empire, 2003.

Cavanah, Frances. *The Truth About the Man Behind the Book that Sparked the War Between the States*. Philadelphia: Westminster Press, 1975.

Charles H. Wright Museum of African American History. "The Dawn Settlement." http://ugrr.thewright.org/media/Pdf/Dawn_Settlement_Communities_UGRR.

Coady, Jean Howerton. "Daviess Countians Claim 'Uncle Tom' as One of Their Own." *Courier-Journal*, September 17, 1979. Accessed via Newspapers.com.

Cohen, Anthony. *The Underground Railroad in Montgomery County, Maryland: A History and Driving Guide*. Rockville, MD: Montgomery County Historical Society, 1994.

Colored Conventions. "Bringing Nineteenth-Century Black Organization to Digital Life." http://coloredconventions.org/items/show/264.

Craig, Berry. "Kentucky Slave Inspired Stowe Novel." *Courier-Journal*, August 11, 1998. Accessed via Newspapers.com.

Daviess County, Kentucky: Celebrating Our Heritage, 1815–2015. Evansville, IN: M.T. Publishing Company, 2015.

Dictionary of Canadian Biography. "Scoble, John." http://www.biographi.ca/en/bio/scoble_john.

Douglass, Ann. "Introduction." *Uncle Tom's Cabin or, Life Among the Lowly*. Boston: John P. Jewett and Company, 1852. Reprint, London: Penguin Books, 1986.

Douglass, Frederick. *Life and Times of Frederick Douglass: His Early Life as a Slave, His Escape from Bondage, and His Complete History to the Present Time*. Hartford, CN: Park Publishing Company, 1881. http:/docsouth.unc.neh/douglasslife/douglass.html.

———. *Narrative of the Life of Frederick Douglass*. Clayton, DE: Prestwick House Literary Touchstone Classics. Unabridged republication, 2004.

Eastern Illinois University. "Underground Railroad: A Path of Freedom." www.eiu.edu/eiutps/undeground_railroad.php.

Francis, Azra D. *Josiah Henson: A Documentary Drama*. Windsor, Ontario: Windsor Italo-Canadian Culture Center, 1988.

Frick, John. "Uncle Tom's Cabin on the Antebellum Stage." *Uncle Tom's Cabin and American Culture*. University of Virginia. http://utc.iath.virginia.edu/interpret/exhibits/frick.

Froehlich, William. "Proclamation of Recognition." Kentucky Room, Daviess County Library.

Hager, Frankie. "Uncle Tom Lived in Daviess." *Messenger Inquirer*, October 22, 1967. Accessed via Newpapers.com.

Harriet Beecher Stowe Center. www.harrietbeecherstowecenter.org/hbs.

Heim, Joe. "In Search of 'Uncle Tom.'" *Washington Post*, June 16, 2016, B1–2.

Henson, Josiah. *The Autobiography of Josiah Henson, an Inspiration for Harriet Beecher Stowe's Uncle Tom's Cabin.* Edited by John Lobb. London, Ontario: Schuyler, Smith & Company, 1881. Reprint, Courier Corporation, 2003.

———. *The Life of Josiah Henson, Formerly a Slave, Now an Inhabitant of Canada, as Narrated by Himself.* Boston: Arthur D. Phelps, 1849. Reprint, Dresden, Ontario: Observer Press, for Uncle Tom's Cabin Historic Site, 1965.

———. *Truth Stranger than Fiction: Father Henson's Story of His Own Life.* Introduction by Harriet Beecher Stowe. Boston: John P. Jewett, 1858. Reprint, New York: Barnes & Noble, 2008.

———. *Uncle Tom's Story of His Life: An Autobiography of the Rev. Josiah Henson (Mrs. Harriet Beecher Stowe's "Uncle Tom").* Edited by John Lobb. London: Christian Age Office, 1876.

Henson Nevels Family. "Last Will and Testament of Josiah Henson." http://hensonnevelsfamily.com.

A History of Daviess County, Kentucky, Together with Sketches of Its Cities, Villages, and Townships, Educational Religious, Civil Military, and Political History, Portraits of Prominent Persons, Biographies of Representative Citizens, and an Outline History of Kentucky. Chicago: Interstate Publishing, 1883. Reproduction, Unigraphic, Evansville, Indiana, 1966.

Illustrated News. "Lost Museum Archive, Uncle Tom's Cabin at Barnum's Museum." November 26, 1853. https://lostmuseum.cuny.edu/archive/uncle-toms-cabin-at-barnums-museum.

John Milner Associates. *Historical Structure Report for the Riley House/Josiah Henson Site.* Montgomery Parks, Montgomery County, Maryland, 2008. https://www.montgomeryparks.org/uploads/2016/07/henson_historic_structures_report-web.pdf.

Kaplan-Levenson, Laine. "Sighting the Sites of the New Orleans Slave Trade." New Orleans Public Radio, WWNO, November 5, 2015. http://wwno.org/post/sighting-sites-new-orleans-slave-trade.

Katz, Sidney. "Jim Crow Lives in Dresden." *Macleans*, November 1, 1949.

King, Julia, Christine Arnold-Lourie and Susan Shaffer. *Pathways to History: Charles County, Maryland, 1658–2008.* Mount Victoria, MD: Smallwood Foundation Inc., 2008.

Klapthor, Margaret Brown, and Paul Dennis Brown. *The History of Charles County Maryland, Written on Its Tercentenary Year of 1958.* Facsimile reprint. Westminster, MD, 2009.

Larson, Kate Clifford. "Bound for the Promised Land: Harriet Tubman, Portrait of an American Hero." Harriet Tubman Biography. http://www.harriettubmanbiography.com/harriet-tubman-myths-and-facts.

Lawrence, Keith. "Memory of Henson's Life Is Fading in Daviess County." *Messenger Inquirer*, August 30, 2017. http://www.messenger-inquirer.com/news/local/memory-of-henson-s-life-is-fading-in-daviess-county/article.

Lee, Jean B. *The Price of Nationhood: the American Revolution in Charles County*. New York: W.W. Norton & Company, 1994.

Lenhart, Jennifer. "'Uncle Tom's Cabin' Will Open to Visitors." *Washington Post*, June 15, 2006. http://www.washingtonpost.com.

The Liberator. "John Scoble." July 2, 1852. Accessed via Newspapers.com.

———. "Josiah Henson—Caution." April, 11, 1851, 4. Accessed via Newspapers.com.

London Times. "Obituary." May 23, 1883, 10. Accessed via Newspapers.com.

Longfellow, Samuel, ed. *The Life of Henry Wadsworth Longfellow*. Vol. 2. https://books.google.com/books?isbn=1591070384.

National Registry of Historic Properties, La Grange. Maryland Inventory, CH3. https://mht.maryland.gov/secure/medusa/PDF/Charles/CH-3.pdf.

Pope, John. "Slave Trade in New Orleans Was a Thriving Business." NOLA News, April 13, 2010. www.nola.com/politics/index.ssf/2010/04/slave_trade_in_new_orleans.htm.

Reynolds, David S. "Rescuing the Real Uncle Tom." *New York Times*, June 13, 2011. http://www.nytimes.com/2011/06/14/opinion/14Reynolds.html.

Rivoire, J. Richard. *Home Places: Traditional Domestic Architecture of Charles County, Maryland*. La Plata: Maryland Studies Center, Charles County Community College, 1990.

Robbins, Hollis. "Uncle Tom's Cabin and the Matter of Influence," The Gilder Lehrman Institute of American History. https://www.gilderlehrman.org/history-by-era/literature-and-language-arts/essays/uncle-tom's-cabin-and-matter-influence.

Russell, Hilary. "Underground Railroad Activities in Washington, D.C." Latin American Studies. www.latinamericanstudies.org/slavery/WH-2001.

Shin, Annys. "After Buying Historic Home, Md. Officials Find It Wasn't Really Uncle Tom's Cabin." *Washington Post*, October 3, 2010.

Shulins, Nancy. "Area Man Leads Fight to Recognize 'Uncle Tom' Link." *The Gleaner*, September 21, 1980, 3.

Siebert, Wilbur H. *The Underground Railroad from Slavery to Freedom: A Comprehensive History*. New York: McMillan, 1898. Reprint, Dover Publications, 2006.

"Si Henson, the Original of Mrs. Stowe's Great Novel." Reprinted in the *Owensboro Messenger & Examiner*, September 10, 1884.

Stevens, Kathleen. *William Still and the Underground Railroad*. West Berlin, NJ: Townsend Press, 2008.

Still, William. *The Underground Railroad*. Philadelphia, 1872. Reprint, Oxford: Benediction Classics, 2008.

Stowe, Harriet Beecher. *A Key to Uncle Tom's Cabin*. Boston: John P. Jewett and Company, 1853. Reprint, Dover Publications, 2015.

———. "The Original Uncle Tom." Reprinted in (Emporia, KS) *Evening News*, August 10, 1882, 2. Accessed via Newspapers.com.

———. *Uncle Tom's Cabin or, Life Among the Lowly*. Introduction by Ann Douglass. Boston: John P. Jewett and Company, 1852. Reprint, London: Penguin Books, 1986.

Tobin, Jacqueline L., with Hettie Jones. *Midnight to Dawn: The Last Tracks of the Underground Railroad*. New York: Anchor Books, 2007.

Uncle Tom's Cabin Historic Site. www.heritagetrust.on.ca/en/index.php/ properties/uncle-toms-cabin.

Underground Railroad. Official National Park Handbook. Washington, D.C.: National Park Service, 1997.

Webster, Rebecca, et al. "In Search of Josiah Henson's Birthplace: Archaeological Investigations at La Grange Near Port Tobacco, Maryland. St. Mary's College of Maryland." 2017 (unpublished).

Wilson, Hiram. "The Letters of Hiram Wilson." https://hiramwilson. wordpress.com.

Winks, Robin. "Introduction." *An Autobiography of Josiah Henson, an Inspiration for Harriet Beecher Stowe's Uncle Tom's Cabin*. Edited by John Lobb. London, Ontario: Schuyler, Smith & Company, 1881. Reprint, Courier Corporation, 2003.

INDEX

ABOUT THE AUTHOR

Edna M. Troiano, who holds a PhD in comparative literature, is Professor Emerita from the College of Southern Maryland, where she chaired the Department of Languages and Literature from 1986 to 2006. She coauthored two college rhetoric texts (*Write to Know* and *The Contemporary Writer*) and coedited an anthology of Christmas literature (*The Roads from Bethlehem*). Her articles, book reviews, and essays have been published widely in academic journals and popular magazines. She lives in Maryland with her husband, Pete; her son, Leo; and her brilliant and beautiful golden retriever, Penelope.

Visit us at
www.historypress.com